LIVE FROM THE OTHER SIDE!

MAUREEN MCGILL AND NOLA DAVIS

OZARK MOUNTAIN PUBLISHING

PO Box 754, Huntsville, AR 72740
479-738-2348 or 800-935-0045; fax 479-738-2448
www.ozarkmt.com

For permission, serialization, condensation, adaptions, or for our catalog of other publications, write to Ozark Mountain Publishing, Inc., P.O. box 754, Huntsville, AR 72740, ATTN: Permissions Department.

Library of Congress Cataloging-in-Publication Data
McGill, Maureen, 1952 -, Davis, Nola, 1956 -
   Live From the Other Side, by Maureen McGill and Nola Davis
A collection of real life stories and ways to connect with the other side - the spirit world.

1. Spirit World   2. Death   3. Metaphysics   4. After-life experiences
I. McGill, Maureen, 1952 -   II. Davis, Nola, 1956 -   III. Life After Death
IV. Spirit World   V. Title

Library of Congress Catalog Card Number:2010933323

ISBN: 978-1-886940-71-0

Cover Art and Layout: www.enki3d.com
Book set in: Times New Roman, Baskerville Old Face, BernhardModBT
Book Design: Julia Degan

Published by:

OZARK
MOUNTAIN
PUBLISHING
PO Box 754
Huntsville, AR 72740

WWW.OZARKMT.COM
Printed in the United States of America

Dedication

To our loved ones in the light, Michael McGill,
Amy Ensley and our parents.

Acknowledgments

Val Dumond, Molly McHugh, Ava Seal, Ann Hart,
Bayly Miller, Sandy Nelson, Joshua Davis and his family

And To
Those who have gone before us and to those who have
contributed their story to this book.

Table of Contents

INTRODUCTION

Your life seems to be moving in the right direction. The sun rises each morning and sets each evening while you race around attending to all that important stuff you need to accomplish. You eat occasionally, pay bills, go to work, pick up the dry cleaning...then it happens. Your cell phone rings, or perhaps there's a knock at the door, and you find a strange someone standing there. Worse yet is when you are handed a note that says, "Please call home immediately!"

It feels as though time has stopped while you dial your phone. Thoughts rush through your head. Is something wrong? Has someone died? What catastrophe has hit? A strange voice answers your phone call. At that moment Death rocks your world. Welcome to Death. Numbness takes over, and you feel like time has stopped. Days pass; months pass, perhaps years. Then strange events begin to occur. Welcome to life from the other side!

You have just been thrown into a new reality show. It begins with you noticing the lamp flicker on and off. You check the bulb and it appears to be working just fine. What is wrong? It never dawns on you that this was Mom's favorite lamp, and that perhaps she is trying to send you a message. Don't you remember walking back into the house after the funeral? When you looked up and said, "Mom, I hope you are okay because I'm certainly not! Give me a sign to let me know you are okay."

You never thought when you voiced those words that Mom would actually give you a sign. Then it happens. How weird is that? Who do you tell? Are you crazy? What now? Why do some people get these messages and others don't?

The book is written to help you answer these questions. The work of the authors in healthcare, university teaching, and the healing arts forms a strong belief in a universal connection. This universal connection is love, the sacred thread Maureen has collected stories from those who have lost loved ones and those who desire communication with them. Using intuition as a guidance tool, she has spoken to those who have shared their encounters with deceased loved ones. Maureen works as an Associate Professor at Pacific Lutheran University in Tacoma, Washington.

Nola has spent over thirty years working in senior healthcare, helping loved ones understand the path of letting go of their dying family members and resolving grief. She works as a corporate executive for a healthcare corporation in Tacoma, Washington. The experiences of those who shared their stories and our own experiences helped us to understand our own intuitive gifts. This became the impetus to helping others. This book represents the fruit of our work.

We believe the threads of love become the pathway through which we communicate to those who have passed. This collection of real stories demonstrates that communication does continue beyond death. We give and receive messages all the time from those who have only left us in body. What follows are real stories from real people.

Into this world we are born,

unable to speak,

yet able to feel,

able to sense.

Within our lives we will learn

to speak, but will we ever

come to know?

From this world we will depart,

unable to speak

still able to feel,

able to sense,

and then we shall know.

-Nola Davis

CHAPTER 1:

HELLO, ARE YOU THERE?

You have survived death. The funeral is over, and you try to move through each day as if nothing happened. You may wonder where your loved one is. You might wish they would give you a sign. You wish there would be something you'd recognize as a sign. Time passes. It happens. The message comes when you least expect it.

SUSAN'S STORY

Susan remembers the experience she had one night in 1962. She was eight years old and had just been tucked into bed for the night. In the dark, she became aware of a circle of light on her bedroom curtains. The light appeared to be coming from the outside, and she thought her brothers were playing a trick on her.

Susan jumped out of bed and went to her brothers' bedroom. A quick check showed they were sound asleep.

She returned to her bedroom, a bit frightened but curious. The circle of light was still there. Susan rationalized that the light could be coming from next door. However, she realized the neighboring house did not have windows on that side. Susan jumped into bed, pulled the covers over her head, and prayed for the circle of light to disappear.

A few moments later, she peeked out from under the covers. Her prayer had been answered, sort of. The circle of light was gone, and in its place was a lovely woman with a kind and gentle face sitting on the twin bed under the window. Susan instantly felt calm, sat up, and stared at the woman.

Although the woman did not speak, Susan could hear words inside her head. As the words formed, she felt peaceful.

The woman spoke, "I am always with you and I love you very much. I am so happy that you are your mother's daughter. Your mother needs you very much."

Susan asked, "Who are you?" In response she heard over and over the name Faith.

Faith told Susan she would feel better soon and not to be afraid. Susan became aware of how Faith was seated on the bed. She had her right leg crossed over her left knee and supported herself by leaning against her right arm. She held a strand of her hair in her left hand and was twisting it, her hand cocked in a certain way.

Faith told Susan that whenever she saw a rainbow she would know that Faith was with her, loving and guiding her. Faith's form seemed to fade away slowly. Susan became fearful, grabbed her blanket, and ran down the hallway to her parents' bedroom.

Susan ran in, calling out that a woman had been in her room. As she described Faith, she sat on the bed the way Faith had been sitting and twisting her hair.

Her mother's face turned pale. She sat up in bed and said, "Jack, look at her! Look at what Susan is doing." Her father looked over and didn't seem the least bit interested. Susan told her mother how Faith had said, "I am always with you and I love you very much."

Her mother started to cry. Her father got up from bed and with an impatient mutter said, "Oh, for Christ sakes," and left the room.

The mother took her daughter back to her own bedroom and asked Susan to show her where the lady had been sitting. Her mother noticed an object on the bed and when she picked it up, her hands began to shake.

The object was a locket that Susan found while exploring the contents of a cedar trunk in her room a few days earlier. Her mother asked, "Where did you find the locket?"

Susan thought she was in trouble but explained, "I was

borrowing it because I thought the lady in the locket was beautiful."

"That's my mother. That's my mother, Faye! It's your Grandmother Faye. She used to sit and twist her hair exactly the way you just did when she was talking or thinking."

Susan's mother was crying as she brought the locket over to Susan. She sat down beside her daughter opened the locket and looked at the beautiful picture inside. She put her arm around Susan and began to rock her gently while continuing to cry.

Susan looked up and asked, "Am I in trouble?"

"No honey, I am not mad at you. Her name was Faye, not Faith. She died when I was 14 years old."

Susan's story illustrates it can be another family member who receives the message. Susan became the messenger for her grandmother's unending love. It doesn't always take a woman sitting on the bed; it could be something a little more subtle. Their visits are surprising. Sometimes the light comes on. Nobody's home, but where are you?

VICKI'S STORY

During the day Vicki worked as a staffing coordinator for a nursing home. In the evenings, she took care of her aging mother. Day in and day out, this was her routine until the day her mother died, leaving Vicki to fill the empty moments. Time passed before Vicki began to go through her mother's belongings. One evening she was sorting things in the bedroom. The lamp began to flicker as if someone was turning it on and off. Vicki had just changed the bulb and noticed that none of the other lights were flickering. She felt so scared that she left the room and closed the door.

A few days later, Vicki told friends at work about the flickering lamp and how frightened she had been. One friend said, "Perhaps this is your mother's way of letting you know she was there, and that she was okay."

"I never really thought of it that way," Vicki replied.

Her friend said, "It is not unusual for us to get some type of message from a loved one. Ask your mom if she is trying to let you know she is here. Tell her not to do anything that would frighten you."

Vicki did as her friend suggested. "Don't scare me mom, but send me a message you are here".

The weeks passed. The lamp never flickered again, and Vicki was at peace.

When you ask someone to give you a sign they are okay, be specific to them about how you want this sign to come. This is a new process for you and for them. They are in a different dimension than you are. Remember, it may take them some time to give you a sign.

It is our belief that when we leave this body we become incarnate and recognize that we are spiritual beings. As spiritual beings we exist in a different dimension composed of energy. Like energy is attracted to like energy. It is like an electrical impulse. Electricity runs at a much higher frequency than the human body. Often electrical frequency seems to be one of the modes for individuals on the other side to contact us. Lights, lamps, radios, televisions, and cell phones compose spiritual contact 101.

Grief can hold you captive. These emotions require a lot of energy. Most of us have seen individuals who become absolutely exhausted because they are so bound by their grief. Remember, the other side connects with grief energetically. Grieving sends a message of loss. When you hold those feelings of loss, and you want someone to let you know they are okay, that is a conflicting message. If you say, "Joe is dead," but then you ask, "Hey, Joe! Give me a sign that you are okay." Did you realize how crazy that is? Grief has a lower vibration. Conflicting messages do not help you to connect. You are sending two different messages: one of loss and one of a desire to connect.

The energetic pull to connect can be very strong for those in spirit. Speak from your heart to them, remembering how they were when they were alive, in the physical. Think about what they were like, the type of person they were. Did they play jokes on people? Did they have a sense of humor? How did you communicate with that person?

It is okay to talk to them as if they are in the physical form standing right in front of you. One of the ways to relate feelings is through words. Share your words and your heartfelt love for this person. Your words are energy. Your words are your calling card to the universe. Use them carefully and be ready for an answer.

AL AND JILL'S STORY

Al's mother Maren was diagnosed with breast cancer. Al and his wife Jill would visit and care for Maren. It was a long battle, and even near the end Maren struggled with staying or dying. Al was advised by the caregivers to tell his mother it was okay to go. She passed away shortly after receiving his permission.

It is not uncommon for our loved ones to wait for us to give them permission to die. They have loved us, nurtured us and cared for us our whole life. When we say, "Mom, it is okay for you to go," there is something that is released emotionally for her. This loving message helps her to release from this physical level of being.

Six months after Maren's death, Al and Jill's daughter, Mia, went to the family cabin for a vacation. The cabin was in the country, a perfect location for rest and relaxation. It had not been used in several months. When Mia entered the cabin she could smell the fresh fragrance of Georgio perfume. She had given her grandmother Georgio perfume as a gift. This fragrance was Maren's favorite; she wore it often. Mia knew this was a sign from her grandmother that she was there with her.

Six weeks later Mia's parents went to the cabin for a

quiet retreat. They were not greeted by the smell of Georgio perfume upon their arrival as Mia had. However, that night, sometime after Al and Jill had gone to sleep, Jill woke up suddenly and realized the bedroom was infused with Georgio perfume. She sat up in bed knowing that her mother-in-law was in the room. Jill did not like the fact her mother-in-law had come to visit in their bedroom and said emphatically, "Maren, you don't have to worry, we are just fine." Jill knew it was important to reassure Maren.

Jill was clearly able to let Maren know they were okay. Her carefully chosen words conveyed what she felt.

When?

When will you come to me?
Will I hear you speak?
Will I know it is you?
Will your visit bring me peace?
When will you ever come to me?
Will I chance to see
That part of you,
you left with me,
That part that I now seek ?
- Nola Davis

CHAPTER 2:

WHO IS SPEAKING?

Have you ever had a day when you learned something new or had an experience you wanted to share with someone? You picked up the phone, called your family and your friends, but no one answered. So, you left a message for them to call you when they have a spare moment.

The need to share your experience reached an all- time high as you stood in line at the latte kiosk. Out of the blue, the person standing behind you started to talk to you. The conversation eventually evolved until you ended up sharing with them what you had wanted to share with your family.

Take this a step further. A loved one has died. They want to communicate with you, but you cannot hear their message. However, someone else does!

BURY ME RIGHT

Edith was born on the Windriver Northern Arapaho Reservation in Wyoming. Life on the reservation was very difficult. Many of the people lived at below-poverty levels with few jobs available for young people. Windriver had very little to offer Edith as she entered into the early years of her adult life. She made the decision that she was going to move to Washington State and build a career for herself. Edith went to nursing school and became a nurse, soon married and raised five children.

Eventually Edith ended up divorcing. The highlight of her life was her four daughters and one son. The daughters were all very close to each other and spent time encouraging their mother to join them on short trips and vacations. She frequently participated, and as she aged, represented a true matriarch of the family.

It was in December of the year prior to her passing when the girls began to notice their mother was losing weight. Months went by before she finally sought medical attention. The days of medical testing began. The test results indicated pancreatic cancer.

Edith's health declined very rapidly. She was hospitalized within a few days. Her brothers who lived on the reservation were notified they needed to come as soon as possible. Edith and her children made the decision to utilize hospice services. Each of the daughters took turns taking care of her mother in her final days. The dying woman was supported and surrounded by her children in the comfort of her own home.

Her brothers arrived just in time to see Edith one last time before she died. The Arapaho tradition of holding the sacred space began with the calling of the elders to come and take their sister home. Edith's house was located near train tracks. The train passed by the house frequently throughout the day. It was early in the morning on the day she passed when the sound of a train approaching inspired her daughters to say, "Go ahead, Mom, get on board the train." Edith took her last breath as the train passed by her house.

One of Edith's daughters was a friend of Nola's. Nola had met Edith only once in her life. Two days prior to Edith's passing, Nola was sitting in her living room at home. She looked up when she heard a female voice say, "Bury me right!" The voice repeated this statement twice. Nola had a vision of a bouquet of yellow roses lying on the ground in a stark area with dust blowing around the roses. She didn't understand the meaning either of what she saw nor the message, "Bury me right!" Edith died two days after Nola's vision; it was clear the roses Nola had seen represented a funeral.

Arapaho tradition requires the remains of the body to be returned to the sacred burial grounds. Edith had wanted to be cremated and had given her daughters specific instructions. She did not want her ashes interred on the reservation in Wyoming. Against her wishes, Edith's siblings persuaded the daughters into burying their mother on the reservation.

A few months after her death, her daughters took the ashes back to the reservation. There is a tradition at the end of the burial ceremony in which the youngest members of the family are to remove all small rocks from the surface dirt on the grave. Once this was completed, yellow roses were laid upon Edith's grave. A strong wind came up, and a storm began to blow dust and dirt everywhere. Her children knew this was their mother's way of letting them know they had not followed her wishes.

Knowing how their mother loved the ocean, the daughters took her remaining ashes there on the second anniversary of Edith's death. The girls rented a condominium on the beach. One of the daughters was in the bathroom when she looked into the mirror and saw her mother's reflection. She immediately rushed out of the bathroom and told her sisters what had just occurred; the visit had startled her. The sisters all agreed their mom's visit was a sign that her final wishes had been met.

EDITH SENDS ANOTHER MESSAGE

Several months following Edith's death, her daughters began looking for their mother's wedding ring. They had looked everywhere and were beginning to fear the ring had been stolen. One of the daughters came to Nola and told her about the missing ring. Edith once again appeared in a vision to Nola. This time, Edith held out a box to her, opened the lid, and there was the long-sought-after ring. The box appeared to look like a sewing box. Nola shared a description of the box with one of Edith's daughters.

A few days later the daughters resumed their search for the ring. Nola's vision directed them to look into their mother's bead box, where they found the ring. The girls were relieved to know the ring had not been stolen.

Loved ones may attempt to communicate to you in different ways. This communication can be through visions, dreams, words, symbols of nature, sounds, smells, and touch. Spirits have already experienced this world. They will communicate with you when the energy of the moment is right. When you have encounters with a spirit, spend some time integrating your experience. You are never alone. Encounters with those who have passed away are more common than you think. When it feels right, share your experiences with someone.

CAROL'S STORY

Many articles and some books have addressed the effects of long term chronic illnesses and the issues spouses encounter. Occasionally, there are spouses who come forth and acknowledge the loneliness they have felt through their spouse's illness. Likewise, the spouse suffering from the chronic illness loves his/her spouse so much that he/she does not want the surviving spouse to be alone. These conversations are often held between the two and not readily shared within the family. This often results in friends and family members garnering opinions that are not necessarily the truth. Who are we to question? Why wouldn't you want the best for someone you have loved your whole life?

Carol and John were married ten years before he was first diagnosed with Parkinson's disease. The progression of the disease caused a loss of physical intimacy between them. Intimacy was a very important part of their marriage. The functional loss combined with the emotions around the illness brought increasing challenges for this couple. Despite the challenges around the disease, the couple remained together for another fifteen years.

It is not uncommon for chronic illness to result in

tremendous financial burdens. In an effort to resolve insurance problems, John and Carol were forced to divorce after twenty-five years of marriage. John wanted to be assured that Carol would be okay after he died. It was important for him to know she had someone in her life that loved and supported her as much as he had.

It was shortly before the divorce when John encouraged Carol to begin communicating with his brother Peter who was in a similar situation with his wife Millie. She was suffering from advanced stages of multiple sclerosis, and the disease had progressed to the point she could no longer speak. Carol and Peter quickly became pen pals, finding common ground through their spouses' illnesses. Over time this became the basis for the start of new love in both their lives. It wasn't long after the new relationship began that John passed away.

Peter wanted Carol to move to Montana where he lived. Carol, out of respect for Millie, did not want to make the move to Montana until Millie had passed away. She also needed to sell her own home in Washington.

Carol finally moved to Montana to be with Peter after Millie's death. The combining of two households led Carol to help Peter sort through Millie's closets. Many of Millie's clothes still had the tags on them and had never been worn. They decided it might be practical to see if one of Carol's close friends back in Washington might want to wear some of these clothes.

On Carol's next trip back to Washington, she brought some of the clothes for her friend Connie, carrying them in a red wardrobe bag. When Connie's husband came home from work and found Lexi, their dog, barking at the red wardrobe bag, he put the bag in the closet, hoping to calm the dog.

A week passed and Connie had forgotten about the bag stored in the closet. One Saturday evening, the dog lay under the couch waiting for Connie to settle down for the night. She was folding towels in the dining room when all of a sudden, Lexi ran out from underneath the couch, running so fast she skidded on the kitchen floor. Lexi only does this if someone she doesn't know comes into the house. She ran under the desk in the office, shaking in fear. Connie walked into the living room, heard nothing and looked around. She sensed heaviness in the air.

She had just started down the hallway when she felt an angry woman say, "I want my clothes back!" Connie didn't hear the voice out loud, but she distinctly heard the words. "I want my clothes back! I want my clothes back!" The voice repeated this over and over.

Connie reacted by saying, "What? Excuse me? What? Oh My God!" Then she remembered the red wardrobe bag in the closet. "Millie, is that you?"

Millie didn't say yes or no. She just said, "I want my clothes back."

Connie instantly, without thinking, said, "Millie, you are free now; you don't need these clothes. These clothes are going to be a blessing for those who do need them. Don't you want to help people?"

Connie felt no response from Millie. She sensed the need to recite a prayer aloud. This prayer encouraged Millie to free herself from this earthly plain and to be one with her higher self. She asked Millie to go to the light.

The next day Connie removed the bag from the apartment, and the room felt lighter. She was checking her emails the same day and received one email from someone she did not recognize. It was one of those forwarded emails with an icon of iridescent flowers. Normally she would not open this type of email. However the subject line caught her eye. It read, "For a friend. I hope the flowers came through. They are so beautiful. Thank you for all your help." The name of the sender was Millie.

Connie was present enough in the moment to sense the heaviness in the air and to feel Millie's anger and her words. Often communication with those who have passed comes when we least expect it. Connie was able to connect to her heart center and speak clearly from her heart to Millie. This connection helped her to acknowledge Millie's presence and help her spirit move to the light. Connie's intention of giving the clothes to those in need was heard and felt by Millie. It is important to remember intention. This intention carried the energy of Connie's words to Millie.

Electronic devices seem to be one of the easiest mechanisms used by those on the other side. Received emails from those who have passed, cell phones ringing, text messages, televisions turning on and off, can all be ways the other side communicates to us. Strange as it may seem, the world of spirit gravitates to using these devices.

COMING BACK SOMEDAY

Katherine and Gregory lived in Washington, D.C. with their two daughters. They spent their summer vacations driving across the country to visit Katherine's relatives in the Pacific Northwest.

One of their favorite memories was driving across the Columbia River Bridge. Gregory would say to them, "Be quiet. We are coming up to the border of Washington State." He would begin singing his favorite song, *Blue Bayou*, made famous by Linda Ronstad.

Katherine and Gregory were married nineteen years when Gregory was first diagnosed with a rare heart disease. He was the love of Katherine's life. He was romantic, spontaneous, and loved to read and travel. When she speaks of Gregory to this day, you can see the special love they had for each other in her eyes. He had been sick for over four years. Greg was a candidate for a heart transplant, but he died two days before the scheduled surgery. He loved the beauty of the Northwest, and Katherine made the decision to have him buried in Washington State.

Katherine and the girls drove across the country for Gregory's internment.

There was a strange occurrence when they drove once again over the Columbia River Bridge. The car radio began playing *Blue Bayou* as they reached the middle of the bridge. The girls and Katherine became dead silent. Katherine knew in her heart this was a clear message from Gregory that he was still with them.

Those that have passed away can continue to share in an event that was important to them when they were alive. The song on the radio was the connection for all the family. The energy of the song connected their souls to Gregory's soul. The timing of the song as they crossed the bridge once again was Gregory's means (the conduit) of conveying to them his everlasting love.

Now and Forever

We hear their voices in the morning and in the night.
They feel our longing and touch our hearts in dreams and songs.
Our restless slumber wakes to new conscious ways.
Love crosses no boundaries as time moves from place to place.
Memories float like rivers of light, unending messages of love.

- Maureen McGill

CHAPTER 3:

WHAT DID YOU SAY?

How many times in your life have you needed to turn and say to someone, "What did you say?" Were you listening to them when they spoke, or were you so busy that you could not hear them? You receive messages and signals in many ways. However, how many messages come your way that you never receive because you are not listening or aware?

Listening isn't always the physical act of hearing. Listening involves sensing and having the desire to be open to information as it comes to you.

KAY'S STORY

Kay was first introduced to Maureen through a mutual friend. She confided in Maureen during their first meeting that her husband had died on Christmas Day. A year later she faced the second loss in her life when her son committed suicide. Two major losses within one year had taken their toll on Kay. She had no desire to go through her husband's and son's personal effects, so she pushed them aside for the time being.

Eventually she made herself begin sorting through her son's belongings. She was in the garage sorting through his effects when she touched her son's old duffle bag. The garage felt cool, and yet, the moment she touched the son's duffle bag, she felt an electrical shock move up her arm and into her shoulder. Kay was surprised. She had touched many of his things while sorting, and this was the only item which had shocked her. She looked for an electrical device that could have produced the shock but found none. She reasoned it wasn't static electricity and decided this was a message from her son, telling her he was nearby.

This experience was important to Kay because she had struggled with her son taking his own life. She deeply felt the message he conveyed to her, which brought her great comfort.

Death is never easy for anyone. Some day each and everyone one of us will face our own death. Every member of a family moves through his/her grieving process in his/her own way. Suicide provides little or no time to prepare for the loss of a loved one. Some family members begin their journey by asking questions why their loved one chose this path or made this choice. They wonder what could they have done to prevent this from occurring?

A family member's grief can become the capsule for closing off the journey to understanding if their grief cannot be resolved. The death of a loved one has nothing to do with what you did or didn't do. Life is sometimes just too hard for people. It is important to remember each soul makes its own journey.

Death is not the end; it is a reawakening for those who commit suicide. It is like going home and being reminded how much you are loved. They have moved out of this body and into a universal consciousness where the emotional burdens of this world no longer weigh them down. They go there to heal and grow in understanding of that part of their journey they could not complete.

AME'S STORY

Ame had been an insulin-dependent diabetic since the age of five. Her medical problems seemed to compound as she aged. By the time she was forty-six years old, life's ups and downs had taken their toll. One spring, she made the decision to move from Washington to California, a decision she made very quickly. All of her support systems and immediate family lived in Washington, yet she did not tell her family what she planned. She left without telling anyone where she was going or making arrangements as to how her physical and medical needs would be met.

Within two weeks of her moving down to California, she was found dead in a hotel room. The coroner's report stated the cause of death was related to her diabetes.

Ame's death left several of her family members asking questions. How did this happen? What could have been done to prevent this? What more could her family have done to support her?

Within one week of her death, Ame's mother had a dream. In the dream she was standing in the middle of a room, and she saw a walnut tree near a window outside of the room. Ame's mother went over to the tree and picked one of the nuts. The nut opened up in the palm of her hand. Out of the nut emerged Ame.

She appeared much younger to her mother; the effects of her diabetes were no longer visible. Ame said to her mother, "I am sorry. This is my fault. I didn't expect things to happen the way they did. I love you!" Ame's mother told her she loved her as well. When her mother woke from the dream, she was ready to share this experience with Ame's siblings, which included Nola. She felt some peace that some of the haunting questions had been put to rest. Ame continues to this day to visit her mother through dreams.

The dream state can provide us with clear connections to those who have passed. Loved ones often look younger and burden-free. Those they have loved who have also passed can be around them, including pets. Pay attention to the dream. Allow yourself to validate your experience. The dream state provides the perfect place for both worlds to meet. Here we are unencumbered by the rational world of our three dimensional living.

Reaching Out
Where are you, I ask every day?
Where is that place that you have gone?
When will I hear your voice?
When will I feel your touch?
How will I know it is you?
Perhaps you are standing near.
-Nola Davis

SEE YOU IN MY DREAMS

Chris was eighteen years old when he died in a tragic car accident. He had been an outstanding student, cross-country athlete and had a large circle of friends. His sister Carey was two years younger. She was struggling with the grief of losing her big brother. It was approximately a year after his passing when Carey had this dream:

"I was standing in my kitchen in the middle of the night. Chris appeared standing at the front door, dressed in a crisp white suit, and he was smiling. It looked like his prom tuxedo, and he was so happy and almost glowing. He looked the same; his hair looked exactly as it did when he was alive, perfectly in place.

"How are you?" he asked.

Carey said, "I'm fine." She knew the minute she said she was fine, she really wasn't okay. At that moment Carey shared, "The sight of him was so uplifting; I just knew he was okay. It was so reassuring to see him so happy."

Carey has had several dreams of Chris over the years. He

18

is always in different places and is curious to know what is going on with her. "There is a part of me that recognizes that he is dead in the dream, but there is also a part of me that knows he is here. One time I saw him in a movie theater, and it was so unexpected. He was just standing behind me and smiling. His visits always make me feel so good. "

Her most recent dream of Chris followed the birth of her first son.

"Hey, how is it going?" Chris asked.

"Oh my gosh," she said. "It has been so long since I have seen you."

"I hugged him and then I woke up suddenly. I could smell him. He wore a particular after shave lotion. I just know he was in the room with me. It was so real."

There are individuals who push aside the very thought of people in the dream state actually having visits from those who have died. People who have visits consistently say over and over how very real it is and the immense sense of joy and relief they feel. Carey found herself in the dream state, realizing on one hand her brother was dead but, on the other hand, she knew he was with her. The intense knowing which surrounded her in the dreams negated any doubts she had carried. Her dream state has become the perfect medium for her brother's visits.

TIM'S VISIT FROM LAURA

Tim was fifty years old when he had the following experience, one he shared only with his wife until now. Three years earlier his neighbors lost their daughter, Laura, at the age of seventeen, from a drug overdose. Tim had four daughters of his own and even though Tim was not very close to Laura, he was saddened by the loss of such a young life.

Approximately three or four weeks after Laura died, Tim was taking garbage out to the back alley behind his home. It was an ordinary northwest day with cool temperatures and cloudy skies. He looked up and saw Laura a few feet away, smiling at him and walking towards her house. Tim described this experience as, "So natural and so real, as if she was truly there. She looked the same; seventeen years old, smiling and wearing her teenage clothes. Laura acknowledged me with her eyes, and I felt very peaceful when I saw her. My first thought was that I wanted to share this with Laura's parents, but I knew I couldn't."

Tim knew Laura's parents were burdened with grief and would not understand his experience. To this day, Tim has not been able to share this experience with Laura's parents.

The first time an individual actually sees a person who has died, they can sometimes experience elation, fear, apprehension, or denial. Her smile, warmth and Tim's interpretation that Laura was okay were all comforting to him. Yet, he remained concerned about sharing this with others.

Each person has to work through a process of separating themselves from doubt and fear. One technique is to sit quietly, set your intention to release all doubt and fear, and ask yourself, 'Why am I doubtful? Why am I fearful?' Pay attention to what you feel or hear after you've asked yourself each question. You may want to write down your responses. This allows you insight into what you have experienced. There is a certain level of vulnerability felt when you share an experience like Tim's. Vulnerability is not necessarily negative in the right context.

Side by Side
They walk down paths, alleys and familiar places.
We see them as real, in youthful faces and strong bodies.
Pain has dissolved, transparent to all we knew.
Smiles and nods fill gaps of time eternal.
Love holds ties forever, side by side.
-Maureen McGill

People are often apprehensive about sharing strange or bizarre experiences. They won't share what happened to them until they can confide in someone they absolutely trust. The process of confiding helps them move through their own doubts and those fears dissolve. Their main concern is what people will think about them once they share their story. It is within this light the next story was shared with us on a warm autumn morning.

UNEXPECTED HELPER

Bart is a police officer in a metropolitan area. Besides his career he enjoys renovating old homes. Two and a half years ago, he purchased his first home, a major remodeling project. The former owner's name was Steven. He had died in a nursing home, and the house remained vacant until Bart purchased it. Steven's son, Tom, lived across the street from his childhood home. Bart felt a need to discuss the changes he was making in remodeling the home. He was sensitive to how the family might feel about the transformation.

A short time after he began the project, Bart began to face some difficulties in the house. His electric power tools would turn off for no reason at all. He was working downstairs when his saw stopped functioning. He went upstairs to check the electricity and what he found was a light fixture which had been unplugged. There were cobwebs all around the light fixture, and there was no trace of anyone who might have touched the fixture. He was dumbfounded and very frustrated. He found himself sitting on a bench and said, "Steve, I just want to get this working. This is my saw, and I just need to get this working." Immediately after he said this, the saw started right up. The power turned back on.

Bart really didn't think anything about this event until it happened again. This time he was putting new trim around the windows. He was using the old trim as a tool for measurement

21

and couldn't make it work; it kept coming up short. This was not like Bart's experience in the past; it had always worked for him and he was really frustrated. Out of nowhere, he said, "Steve, let me get this done." From that moment on, he had no difficulties cutting the trim and installing the windows.

One night Bart was working the night shift patrolling a very large area. It was 3:00 A.M., and he found himself driving alone in an industrial part of town. This was not an area he would necessarily have an interest in patrolling, and he had not been called to investigate any unusual incidents in the area.

He told us out of the blue, "I found myself pulling up in front of a business, which operated twenty- four hours a day. For some unknown reason, I went to the door. Mind you, a patrol officer almost never will enter a building without just cause, but something was calling me to enter. One of the employees welcomed me and seemed bewildered by my presence. It was a machinist factory, where machinists crafted parts for commercial airplanes. The employee gave me a tour, and I never really understood why I stopped there. I found myself fascinated by the level of precision in the manufacturing."

It was a few weeks later when Bart completed the remodeling of the house. He invited the family over to see the changes he had completed. One of the sons was impressed with Bart's work, "You did a fine job with this. Our dad would be impressed. You know, our dad was a perfectionist."

Bart asked, "What was Steve's occupation?"

"Dad was a machinist."

"Where did he work?"

"He worked for a company called Precision Manufacturing, located on the Tide Flats."

Bart knew at that moment why he had stopped his patrol car in the middle of the night. He was convinced Steve was trying to show him where he worked and was giving him permission about the remodeling. Bart felt Steve was acknowledging the quality job he had finished.

This was a phenomenal experience for Bart. He allowed himself to be open and connect to spirit. This allowance provided him with the opportunity to receive guidance, direction and the experience of a lifetime. He was excited to have the opportunity to share his story with us. We asked Bart about the training police officers receive regarding the use of their intuition. Bart said they are taught to always pay attention and be aware of what is around them. His attention to this awareness allowed him to acknowledge Steve's presence.

CHAPTER 4:

OH, THAT CAN'T BE!

Family members often find a certain place or a certain time of the day when they choose to have a conversation with their loved one who has passed. Maybe you are busy preparing dinner. This is the time of the day you always catch yourself talking to your mom. You say, "Mom, I don't know why you can't be like everyone else and give me a sign you are okay." A few minutes later the cooking pot moves across the stove by itself. You scratch your head and say, "Oh, that can't be!"

CHRISTINA'S STORY

Christina met her husband when he was stationed with the military in Germany. After they married he was transferred back to the United States and ended up in Washington State. Friends become like family in the military, and this was the case for Christina and Maria. Maria was French, a cook who enjoyed laughing, visiting, and preparing gourmet meals for her friends. The women and their husbands found many things in common during their evenings around the table. Christina even became the godmother of Maria's two children.

It was one of Christina's favorite things to sit on her back porch and relax on warm summer afternoons. It was an August afternoon when Christina was experiencing severe back pain. She decided to go outside and see if sitting on the porch and relaxing would help the pain to subside. Out of nowhere, she heard her deceased mother say in German, "Don't worry my child; you are going to be okay."

She stood up and felt the need to share her experience

with Maria. Christina told Maria about hearing her mother's voice and what her mother had said to her. Maria was absolutely astounded by what Christina had told her. She could not believe it! They started arguing. Christina insisted over and over again that she had heard her mother's voice. There was nothing that she could say to convince Maria. Maria was exhausted from their arguing and attempted to change the subject by focusing the conversation on Christina's back pain, insisting that she see a physician. Christina took Maria's advice, and the tests results revealed cancer which had metastasized throughout her body.

It was six months later when Christina told Maria that she was at peace with dying, and she wasn't afraid. It took some time for Maria to reflect on Christina's story. Eventually, she found solace in believing Christina's mother's message that she would be okay.

One morning Maria was making breakfast for her two children when she looked up and saw a shadow move past the doorway. The apparition was of a well-dressed woman in a flowing skirt. The woman placed her purse in the bedroom, just as Christina would do. At first, Maria thought it was her daughter playing a trick on her, but she realized her daughter was eating breakfast in the kitchen. Within seconds the phone rang; it was Christina's husband. He told Maria that his beloved wife had just died. Maria knew at that moment the apparition was Christina. She felt deeply touched that her friend had come to say goodbye. Christina's mother's message eventually helped Maria to know her friend was okay.

This experience opened Maria's heart to the possibility of life after death. You may in your lifetime have encounters with non-family members, friends, or even people you don't know very well that have crossed. These encounters can often occur before or at the time you are experiencing difficulties in your life. The difficulties can be physical illness, emotional problems, or financial challenges. These encounters can leave you wondering what this is all about. It is important to remember time only exists in this earthly dimension. Do not try to understand the how or why you receive this information. Just keep your heart open and acknowledge to yourself that when it is the right time, you will know.

CRYSTAL'S STORY

Jaimee served on the board of directors for a Tacoma, Washington homeless shelter that provided food, clothing, and daytime resources. She had met Crystal, age fourteen, at the shelter about twelve years earlier. Crystal's parents had lost custody of Crystal and her brother, who then lived in several foster homes. Crystal encountered many struggles, including the loss of her brother, who was killed in one of the foster care homes.

Jaimee befriended Crystal and even offered to have her live with her if she would go to school and follow some house rules. Although she could not agree to the rules, Crystal did spend occasional evenings at Jaimee's home. Jaimee eventually became like her surrogate mom, taking her to a hairdresser, shopping, and out to restaurants. Jaimee's fondest memories were the meals they had together of cracked crab and popcorn.

Crystal frequented the shelter and hung out with the young people. They were like puppies, clinging to one another for protection. She was the youngest of the pack of kids who lived like gypsies, sleeping in motels, cars, and abandoned buildings. If one of them was lucky enough to get money for an apartment, they would all sleep there until the money ran out.

Crystal was almost sixteen years old when her life became more complicated by pregnancy. She arrived one day at the shelter with a black eye and swollen cheek. The staff at the homeless shelter told Jaimee about Crystal's boyfriend, an ex-convict, prone to violent behavior. When Jaimee found out where Crystal's boyfriend lived, she went to the house and confronted him, saying, "If you hit her again, I will call the police!"

He told Jaimee in broken English that he never hit her and would not admit to the attack. She returned to the shelter knowing she needed to speak with Crystal. She told her emphatically, "No one is allowed to hit you! Get out of this relationship right away."

Crystal shrugged her off with, "He will never hit me again."

A few days later Jaime was attending a meeting at the shelter to identify resources and options available for Crystal. She was encouraged by the outcome of the meeting. Crystal would receive the needed attention and have access to prenatal care. The team recommended a home for unwed mothers versus Crystal staying at the homeless shelter. A social worker from Catholic services came into the meeting room and announced they all needed to go to the chapel. There the shocking news unfolded about Crystal's sudden death. She had been found murdered.

Jaimee was stunned, traumatized by the news. She soon found herself looking down on her own body and screamed in disbelief. A split second later she was back in her body feeling totally disconnected and out of sorts. The murderer was arrested that night and eventually convicted of two counts of second degree manslaughter. He was sentenced to fourteen years in prison. The entire shelter staff grieved deeply over the murder of this young woman.

Crystal was to be buried on the Tulalip Indian Reservation. Jaimee was emotionally exhausted by Crystal's death. The day before the funeral, she decided to lie down and rest on her couch. She heard Crystal's voice say very clearly, "I am here; touch your face."

Jaimee sat up, cupped her hands and lightly tapped her face in the most loving way. She knew she was touching Crystal's face and not her own. Immediately, she realized that it was Crystal and said, "Oh my God, you are okay!"

Jaimee truly believed this was Crystal's way of letting her know she was all right. She wondered for a second if there was something she could do to bring Crystal back to stay longer, but the moment vanished. It was such a magical moment and very real for Jaimee. She wished it had lasted longer. The touching of Crystal's face opened Jaimee's heart to embracing the connection they would always share.

HOUSE OF SPIRIT

When Ray was first diagnosed with Lou Gehrig's disease, none of the family members understood the impact of this disease and the journey they would make together. Ray passed four years later. His wife Patty was devastated by his death; he was her beloved.

Month by month, time passed. She questioned why he had to die so young. One by one, each of his children shared with Patty their encounters with Ray. Patty longed for a visit from him. Why hadn't Ray visited her?

Grief can be a very strong emotion. This emotion binds you to the past and keeps you from living in the present. You can become so busy being absorbed by the emotions of grief that you close your heart to the infinite possibilities. The desire to have a visit conflicted with being distraught over Ray's passing and held Patty hostage.

Patty began to let go of her grief through time. She threw herself into being busy with family and friends. Her encounter with Ray finally occurred one night in her sleep.

She dreamed she was with her entire family, which included her grandchildren. They were standing outside of a house that everyone present knew was haunted. This led Patty to believe that you did not want to be caught inside the house after midnight.

One of the grandchildren had left something related to a school project inside the house. When Patty heard one of her grandchildren say they were not willing to go inside and wanted someone else to go, Patty decided she would go. She entered through the front door. Straight ahead was a door which led to a closet. To her right was a long hallway. She opened the door to the closet and reached inside. She heard the clock chime midnight and became extremely frightened when she sensed a presence approaching her. A feeling of being paralyzed overtook her, and she couldn't move.

Patty turned and saw a figure walking up the hallway. As the figure came closer, she recognized it as Ray, and her fear dissolved. She described him as looking younger and healthy once again. He walked up to her, kissed her on the lips, and told her she was his beloved. She woke up immediately from the dream. The physical contact felt real. Three days later Patty could still feel his kiss upon her lips. To this day she can close her eyes and still feel his kiss.

My Beloved
Dedicated to Patti & Ray

I remember the day you passed.

The thought of losing you was the only thing which filled my mind.

Your passing was my worst fear. I did not understand why you had abandoned me and left me to this world.

At first the sheer silence of the house greeted me each day.

I would lie awake at night wondering where you were and why you had to leave me? The silence of the night brought me no answers — just simple silence. It was within this silence that tears streamed down my face. I explored within myself what it would be like if you were here now, lying with me in the darkness of this night.

Time passed quickly. I kept myself busy each day. The weariness of my day-to-day trivial affairs somehow began to fill the emptiness you left behind. Each day blended into another. The sight of two young lovers brought tears to my eyes. I wanted to say to them, "Be careful! Don't love each other so much. Be careful. Do not let this love fill you up. You have no idea when it is gone what the emptiness will do to you."

I remembered today. It has been over a year since you died. Today I went to your grave. I brought you your favorite flowers. It rained. The rain drops streamed down my face like a final cleansing. I looked up and finally felt the coolness of the rain upon my face. Somehow I had survived it all. This time by myself has taught me many things.

I have come to know a strength I never knew I possessed. All of the things I thought I could or would not ever do, I have done this past year.

I have begun to realize why you loved me. I have begun to realize the faith and belief you held for me. I have come to realize that if you had not died, I might not have ever come to know that very part of myself you admired and loved so much.

You believed in me. You believed in me so much you knew you could depart. You knew I would eventually find the part of myself you had tried so hard to show me. I now understand. The tears streaming down my face no longer come from loss but are tears of love. I finally understand how very much you loved me and will forever love me. Your love comforts me tonight. This precious gift your departure gave to me will always be within me. Thank you, my beloved!

-Nola Davis

CHAPTER 5:

WHY NOT?

Nola has worked many years in the world of healthcare, tending to those in the final years of their lives. No one, no matter how exposed to death, is ever ready when it comes to the departure of loved ones. You can think you are ready, but perhaps this is just the beginning. The death of someone you love can become the greatest journey to understanding life. Living goes beyond this dimension. It extends into all dimensions. This journey moves us into walking side by side with those we love always.

GEORGE'S STORY

George was the father of seven children. His second oldest daughter is Nola. George's mother passed away in the early sixties from cancer. From the moment of her death, George began to worry that he, too, would be a victim of cancer. His son, Clinton, died from cancer at the young age of twelve. This was two years after the passing of George's mother. Immediately he gave up smoking his favorite pipe, one of the few vices he enjoyed of in life. A little over thirty years after his mother's death, George was diagnosed with terminal cancer.

In December while George was visiting his daughter Nola, he made the decision to try chemotherapy treatments even though he was not expected to live another six months. The discussion evolved around the future quality of his life and the potential negative impact of the treatments on his body. Nola felt it was important to talk to her father about being told he was "terminal" and his feelings about death. This was a difficult conversation for her, as she loved her father very much.

She started the conversation by saying, "I can't imagine

how someone works through being terminal and knowing their life is going to end soon."

He looked at her and said, "I have known for some time now that I wasn't going to beat the cancer."

"How did you know this?"

"I was sitting in my chair one Sunday morning about fourteen months ago, looking out the window, when I noticed three people walking up the driveway. Your brother, Clinton, and my two deceased brothers were with him. They walked up the steps and into the house. All of them came and stood in front of me and said nothing. I knew at that moment I would not survive my battle with cancer. I also know they will be with me when the time comes for me to go. This isn't the first time that I have been visited by Clinton."

He then told Nola the story of Clinton's first visit. He talked about how important the visit was to him, that it provided him with an opportunity to tell his son how much he loved him. Father and daughter spent the entire evening talking about these visits and sharing the feelings they both had about his eventual passing. Many tears were shared, and at the same time two hearts were prepared for the transition yet to come.

It was early August the following year when Nola received a telephone call that her father only had a few days left. She loved her dad deeply and had always seen him as a silent strength for herself. The death watch began. Nola had promised her dad she would be there with him when he died. Two days went by. Nola stayed with her dad all day and would only leave late in the evening to get some rest. On Thursday evening, Nola prepared to leave for the night. She kissed her dad good night and told him she loved him.

Nola left her parents' house and went back to her aunt's house where she was staying. Weary from the long hours of sitting, she fell asleep quickly. Nola had an experience similar to a dream. She found herself walking with her dad along the road in front of her grandparents' orchard. Nola and her dad were communicating but not speaking words. They came to a point where she saw an incredible light. She looked closely at the light and saw figures of people. The people were moving forward in the light towards Nola and her dad. The edge of the light appeared to create a line. Nola saw her deceased brother, Clinton, her dad's brother, and his mother. They moved to the edge of the light.

Nola and her dad stopped walking. She turned to her dad and took both of his hands in hers saying, "Dad, they are here, to help you cross. It is not my time. I can't go. I will stay here with you until you are ready to go."

She woke up suddenly to the sound of the phone ringing. It was her mother, calling to let her know her dad had just passed. She knew on some level she had fulfilled the promise she had made to her father, which was to be with him when he crossed over.

Fourteen years later, Nola was lying in bed one night. The following is an account of her experience:

"I was lying in bed thinking about when my father was dying. It was like a movie screen being turned on. I saw the August afternoon again. I could feel how hot the room had been and was once again watching the pain move across his face. He kept reaching out and pointing to something which seemed like it was in front of him, yet so far away. From somewhere came an overwhelming thought, a thought about what it must be like to be physically dying. I could feel his struggle. At some point the struggle of leaving his body shifted into a sense of calm. I knew he had returned home to the place where spirit rejuvenates, rests, and heals from this earth's journey."

"My mind flashed before me the memories of those I have seen as they drew their final breath. Twenty-nine years of working in healthcare brought each face back, one by one. I remember the soft expressions that flood their faces. Their mouths soften, almost in a final effort to say 'Ah, I am done.'"

"I saw my father before me, his struggle of unfulfilled

dreams released. There was the light of hope and joy within his eyes. He looked young again. He no longer pointed at something far away as it was now before him. He came to remind me of the journey that someday all of us will travel."

BUTTERFLIES

Karla's mother-in-law had been diagnosed with cancer. During her illness the hospice workers had built a mobile of colorful butterflies that hung over her bed. Elaine also had a collection of the most beautiful butterfly clips. During the last day of Elaine's life, her daughter Maggie had come to visit. The lavender butterfly clip fell off the mobile and landed on the floor while Maggie was visiting.

Maggie reached down for the fallen lavender butterfly, and Elaine said, "Don't you see the bed is moving?"

Maggie said, "It is okay Mom. The bed is fine. It is not moving!" Maggie clipped the butterfly back onto the mobile. Right before Elaine died a few moments later, the lavender butterfly clip began moving on the mobile while all the other butterflies remained still.

Karla, one of Elaine's daughters-in-law, was still struggling with Elaine's death a few months later. She attended a professional gathering of friends held at Nola's home and brought up her concern about Elaine going to heaven. This concern was based on Karla's theological beliefs. Nola knew nothing about Elaine's life, nor had she ever shared with Karla her gift of clairvoyance. During the evening Nola felt the need to tell Karla what she had begun to see, as Karla discussed her concern about where Elaine would end up.

Nola shared, "I see a very sweet person who is taking her time walking down a road. She has just turned and nodded her head at me. She knows I see her. Now she is raising her hand with her palm in the air. Out of her palm float hundreds of beautiful butterflies, sweeping from small to large with the most delicate wings. The last butterfly floating out of her palm is lavender. Now she is showing me a lavender butterfly that looks like it could be a clip or a pin." Nola turned to Karla and asked, "What is the significance of the lavender butterfly that Elaine keeps showing me floating out of the palm of her hand?" Elaine kept showing Nola this picture over and over. Karla shared the story of Elaine's death and the significance of the lavender butterfly clip to Nola.

Butterflies have been interpreted as symbols of transformation in death by many cultures. The butterfly represents the soul. Elaine opened her hand and the butterflies were released. Elaine was no longer held captive by her illness. Her spirit had been freed. People make certain connections to objects during their life. Those objects can become symbols at the time of death and even after death. They become the calling card to let us know they are present and with us.

THE MATCHMAKER

Lisa, Larry and June graduated from the same high school in 1958. A year later Lisa married and the two couples found themselves living a few blocks away from each other. Lisa and June became best friends, and the two women and their families even shared summer vacations. In 1978, Lisa's marriage began to fail and she separated from her husband. Eventually, they divorced. Larry and June continued to provide emotional support for her during this difficult time. They would include her in all their activities. June was like Lisa's sister, and many people would mistake them as being sisters. June's life changed dramatically in 2004 when she was diagnosed with lung cancer.

Lisa and June shared many conversations during this difficult time. June told Lisa, "I want you to watch over Larry when I am gone."

"I will, June, and anyone that Larry might meet must pass inspection not only by me but from our closest friends."

June also told Larry, "I just want you to be alone for one year, and then I want you to move on and find someone to love. I do not want you to be alone!"

"I don't want to hear this," was Larry's reply.

The friends had their 50th class reunion in the summer of 2008. June attended even though the illness was taking a toll on her. At the event Lisa and June had their picture taken together. When Lisa received the photo, she found a special place on her mantel to display it, a reminder of their close friendship.

It was a slow battle and June did not want to surrender to her illness. Despite her resistance, she lost her battle to cancer in October 2008. June was not alone at her passing; Larry and Lisa were both by her side.

After her death Larry and Lisa would often go out for coffee. Larry found himself surrounded by friends in those early days. Lisa would go home and find herself telling June how much she missed her voice, her face and her presence in her life.

A friend of Larry's invited him to go bowling in hopes this would keep him busy while he was struggling with the loss of his devoted spouse. Larry eventually asked Lisa to join them on Saturday mornings accompanied by his extended family. Leaving Lisa and Larry, the individual who had asked Larry to bowl bowed out of the threesome after a few weeks playing together. After bowling they would go to lunch, and after lunch would often drive to Larry's home, much like they did when June was alive. This routine continued for a few weeks when one Saturday approximately seven months after June's death, Larry confided in Lisa, "I have romantic feelings for you."

Lisa was shocked and had never even considered Larry in that way. Larry was her friend, but he was also the husband of her best friend. Lisa needed to discuss this with her family and ponder this possibility before she could move into something more than a friendship. She took about two weeks to think about this connection with him and realized her feelings were mutual. Lisa decided to share her new found feelings with her family. Her family surprised her by saying they had all realized this connection long before Lisa and Larry were ever aware of it.

They began to see each other more often, dining together, watching movies, and continuing to enjoy conversations. They were moving into a much deeper relationship.   Less than a year after June's passing Larry brought over a picture of June opening a champagne bottle. It had been taken years ago when she was much younger and looked very attractive. Lisa placed the loose photograph next to the framed picture from the class reunion. About a week later Larry brought over a frame for the photo.

Lisa was in the kitchen when Larry called out to her, "Where is the photo I brought over for you?"

"It is on the mantel, next to the framed one" Lisa said.

"No it's not, I don't see them," he said.

When Lisa approached the living room, she was totally startled and could not believe her eyes! The pictures on the mantel had been turned backwards, facing away from the room. "Oh my gosh! No one has been in this house except me. It has to be June! She has been here to visit. If the photos had blown off the mantel, I would have picked them up and faced them into the room. There is no way anyone could have done this, not you or me. No one else has been in the house."

Who could have turned the pictures around? Could it have been June? Was June trying to convey a message to her best friend? Was she upset that Larry had not waited a year before becoming romantically involved with someone? Or did she want to respect their privacy and simply turned the pictures away out of courtesy?

Lisa thought it would be hard for June to watch them together. June had struggled so hard towards the end of her life. She had not wanted to die. Lisa believed June was giving her blessing to them by turning the photos around. She also felt that

June might have a divine hand in bringing them together. Lisa had remained single thirty years after her divorce and had always told June she hoped for a man who possessed high work ethics, was loyal to home, and devoted to family. Her dream had come true and so unexpectedly.

It is not uncommon for couples to be friends. Life events take place bringing the surviving spouses together. The years of friendship and family ties become the foundation for a solid relationship. This is not to say it is easy. Fearing the repercussions, the spouses often will hide their new found love from their family members fearing the repercussions. Each spouse needs to take the time to heal from his/her loss. Spirit has a wonderful way of gently taking our hands and guiding us into the next phase of our lives. Those on the other side who truly love from a space of non-possessiveness will often participate in bringing the two people together. One could say this is their way of blessing the new relationship.

THE FINISH LINE

Gordy was a marathon runner since his college days and had a career as a recreational therapist who devoted his life working with the mentally ill and disabled. He met his wife Shari when they were both teenagers. Together they raised three sons, one who is autistic. Gordy religiously coached Special Olympics in his town and gave many years of leadership and service to this organization.

In his mid-forties he contracted a rare virus which affected his heart. His condition was complicated as a result of being a long distance runner. His heart was enlarged. He began taking a special medication which helped him for a short time. He was feeling better and decided one day to go for a run on his lunch hour with a work colleague.

They had run about a mile when his friend noticed Gordy

had stopped and was gasping for breath which alarmed him. Suddenly Gordy collapsed and his friend ran for help. The paramedics arrived and determined Gordy was in cardiac arrest. They initiated CPR and rushed him to the hospital. They were able to get a heartbeat but Gordy remained non responsive to verbal stimuli.

Shari had been called and headed immediately to the emergency room.

Her heart began to sink. Gordy had always told her, "He would die running." Eventually she was allowed in to see Gordy. She leaned over his bed and said, "Gordy, if you are in pain blink once for no, and twice for yes." His eyes blinked twice. "I love you," she said. That was the last communication between them as Gordy fell into a comatose state.

Shari knew Gordy's wish was not to remain on life support. She also knew he was a universal donor. He wanted to make available anything from his body that could benefit others upon his death. After a couple of days Shari had a final meeting with the family. It was time for her to give permission to pull life support.

Shari went to Gordy's bedside to have a few moments alone with him.

She knew he was struggling. She placed her head on his chest and could feel his heart pounding. She knew it was important for her sons to have a few final moments with their father alone. She left the room and joined her autistic son in the waiting room.

Her two older sons placed their heads on their dad's chest and said goodbye without words. Tim, the autistic son, had been in the waiting area and did not see any of the goodbyes. When Shari came back in the room with Tim she noticed Gordy's color leaving his body. She knew this was the end. Tim on his own went up to his dad's bedside. He placed is face on his dad's cheek so he could feel his breath leaving his dad's body. He kissed his dad. The family was touched by Tim's sensitivity to this loving moment. "I am sure Gordy felt this love in the moment of his passing," Shari said.

Gordy died peacefully with his family surrounding him. This was his wish.

Gordy's life was celebrated at his memorial service. The church was filled with many of the Special Olympics young people who had been touched by his work with them. During the service, the kids lined up and each one placed their precious Olympic medals they had won in competitions in a basket near the altar as a final tribute to Gordy. It was a heartfelt moment for all who attended.

At Gordy's memorial reception Steve, Shari's younger brother, shared this story with her. Steve was not at the hospital when Gordy died. He was at home working on his computer. Their relationship had its ups and downs and they had not been speaking to each other for quite some time. At approximately 6:00 P.M., forty minutes to Gordy's passing, Steve felt Gordy's hand brush his hand. He stopped for a moment at the computer and felt at peace. It was like their disagreement had dissolved with the brush. Steve knew it was Gordy reaching out to him.

Gordy's visit with Steve prior to his actual physical death is not as uncommon as many would think. The desire to resolve unfinished business is often part of the dying process. A soul's final preparation opens the door for these encounters. The intention of a soul to reach out to another soul is extremely powerful. Steve felt Gordy's presence and acknowledged his desire to resolve their differences. Steve was at peace following this encounter. When an individual has an experience like this, it helps them understand their universal connection.

Approximately six months after his death, Shari had a dream. "I was in my family home where I grew up. It was the home I was living in when I met Gordy. I was walking down the driveway and feeling very peaceful. I saw Gordy walking toward the house with his back turned toward me. His hair was long and curly. He never had curly hair." "Gordy, you are here," Shari said aloud. Gordy turned around and his eyes were closed and he looked healthy once again. "Gordy, you can open your eyes," she said. He opened his eyes but they were white. She felt at peace but saddened he did not have his eyes. It is important to note Gordy had donated his corneas to the blind upon his death.

It was a very short time later that Shari's sister had a dream about Gordy. "I was in a huge mansion; it was beautiful with lots of rooms. I could see Gordy walk into the room. He had his back to me. He had thick brown curly long hair, just like your dream! He was beaming, tan and happy when he looked at me."

I asked, "Gordy, Are there angels over there?

"Oh yeah! It is out of this world!" he said.

A year and a half after Gordy died, Shari had yet another visit from him. She had a waking vision; it was that time between waking and sleeping. "I was in the same family home I grew up in. I walked into the house and Gordy was there. I couldn't see his face but I knew he was there. 'Gordy, you are here. Oh, I just want a hug,' I asked him. The next thing I knew I was in bed with Gordy and we were holding each other. 'Your hair is so thick and curly,' I told him. And right between his shoulder blades was one long curl. It felt so real. I knew he was with me."

The curly hair again was seen in this vision, same as her sister had seen many months earlier.

"He comes to me a lot. I hear 'our song' on the radio. I know that Gordy is with me. It is weird; it comes on the radio when I am really feeling down. It just opens my heart. I know he has given me a sign that he is with me. The song is "You're the One." As it goes:

> "You're the One that I long to kiss
> Baby you're the One that I really miss
> You're the One that I'm dream'in of
> Baby you're the One that I love."

(The Vogues, 1965, written by Petula Clark and Tony Hatch)

CHAPTER 6:

WELL, WHO SAID?

Have you ever had such an incredible experience that when you shared it with someone else, they kept telling you, "No way! You must have imagined it."

You reply, "No, I didn't, I know it was real!"

*These **unbelievable** experiences serve as a form of initiation into a new awareness. Some will forever question, while others come to realize the thin veil between other dimensions. Each dimension walks side by side. If you ask, "How do you know this?" We would answer that we know this from what we see, feel and sense.*

We believe we are spiritual beings having an experience on this earth, an experience which provides us opportunities to grow and learn as souls. We are never separate from spirit even when we are incarnate.

CALLER I.D.

Susan and Ann met, and over the course of time they developed a deep relationship with each other. Eventually they became life partners. Through time Susan was diagnosed with breast cancer. It became apparent through the days and weeks to follow that this disease would take her life. As Susan's death neared, her family and friends gathered and were with her when she crossed over. Those present included Ann, Susan's friend John, and Ann's friend Jamee.

At the first year anniversary of Susan's death, an unusual occurrence took place. Jamee called John to make a business appointment.

He answered the phone, saying, "Who is this?"

"This is Jamee."

Disbelief filled his voice as he asked, "Where are you?"

"I'm at home. Why are you asking this?"

"My caller identification indicates that Susan is calling me."

Jamee was stunned by this comment. Approximately a week later, her caller ID also indicated that Susan was calling. Jamee assumed Ann had never disconnected Susan's phone.

Later, when Ann called Jamee, her caller ID indicated once again that Susan was calling her. Jamee asked, "Ann, are you over at Susan's house?"

"No, why would you ask that?" Ann replied,

"My caller ID indicates that Susan is calling me on the phone."

"That phone was disconnected when she died a year ago! I can't believe what is going on! When I spoke to John today over probate matters, he said, 'Hi Ann' and when I asked him how he knew it was me, he said that Susan's name showed on his caller ID. Since Susan was dead, he assumed it was me."

Ann became more upset and repeated, "I am calling you from my house, Jamee. Susan's number was disconnected when she died a year ago."

The situation upset Ann so much that she went to the phone company where the situation became more complex. The phone company informed her Susan's name had never been added to Ann's home phone. After Ann explained to the people at the phone company what had taken place, the phone representative said there was absolutely "no way" this could have happened!

Ann and Jamee discussed what could be the reason for the phone calls. Was Susan trying to communicate with them? Perhaps this was her way of letting those she loved know she was okay. They finally came to the conclusion that this was Susan's way of checking in with them, regardless of what the people at the phone company told them.

DAD'S MESSAGE

Mary Jo was nineteen years old when her dad died unexpectedly at the age of fifty-one. She was close to her dad and felt very saddened by his early death. Mary Jo was contemplating a move to California but had been concerned about how this would impact her mother's life. She eventually decided to move from her family home in Washington to an apartment in Oakland, California, even though it weighed heavily on her mind to leave her mother so shortly after her father's death.

It took some time before Mary Jo began to notice the tenant who lived across the hall. She could see through the glass door on the apartment and noticed this person who lived simply with few furnishings. She learned his name was Peter by checking the mailboxes. Each day she would watch him come and go from the apartment building, always traveling by bicycle. They never spoke.

One day she heard a knock on her door. Peter was standing at the doorway with a friend he introduced as Michael. Out of the blue, Michael said to her, "You are having a hard time with your dad's death. God is not what you think he is, but he is here and your dad is fine. This is too hard for you to understand now. In death, you go to a place and wait to come back." These were his only words. Michael and Peter then turned and walked away.

Mary Jo stood in the doorway and felt an amazing sense of peace knowing her dad was fine. She never saw Michael in the building again. They never spoke again. She felt Michael was a spiritual messenger sent to comfort and assist her through this lonely time.

This was the first of two profound experiences for Mary Jo. The second took place shortly after her mother moved into a new home. A little over a year had elapsed when Mary Jo had a dream one night. In the dream she saw her dad standing at the head of a staircase. He was embracing her mother. Mary Jo had

47

no doubt this was her dad's way of letting her know he was watching over her mother.

Several months later she went to visit her mother in her new home. As she opened the door, she instantly recognized the landing and the staircase. Both were identical to the images she had in her dream. This experience helped Mary Jo to acknowledge the importance of the dream she had many months earlier.

Spirit speaks to us in many ways. It reminds us we are never separate from each other no matter if we are awake or asleep. Mary Jo clearly experienced her dad's spirit in the dream state. She awoke with a knowing so clear and present that it helped her to move forward in the healing of her loss. The visit to her mother's house months later helped to validate the reality of her dream and the strength of her knowing.

HERE'S JOHNNY!

Johnny was a young adult when his mother passed away. She had placed him in a nursing facility prior to her death because she could not care for him. Johnny was developmentally disabled, blind and autistic, but despite these disabilities, he had an incredible gift. His autism enabled him to remember in explicit detail what he heard on television, in stories which were read to him, and information people shared.

Johnny would watch the former talk show host Johnny Carson on television late at night. You may wonder how someone who is blind would watch television. He would sit directly in front of the television, stare at it, and listen intently.

The staff of the facility grew fond of Johnny and became his family upon the death of his mother. The employees engaged in conversations about how to explain the concept of death to Johnny. There were many discussions on what to say to him. The staff decided simply to tell him that his mother had died.

Johnny would always refer to himself in the third person when he spoke about himself. The days following the information of his mother's death led him to rocking back and forth and repeating, "Johnny's mama died. Johnny is sad. Johnny's mama died. Johnny is sad." He said this over and over.

Johnny could not move past the emotion of losing his mother. Nola decided it was the right time to help Johnny move through his loss. The thought came to her to try and help him understand he had not really lost his mama. She said to him, "One day you are going to see your mama again. Dying is like getting on an escalator and riding it all the way to heaven."

His whole demeanor shifted. He smiled and said, "One day Johnny will get onto the escalator and ride it to heaven. One day Johnny will get onto the escalator and ride it to heaven." Over and over he said this. Then out of the blue Johnny said, "Johnny will get off of the escalator and see his mama. Mama will say, "Hereeeeeerrrree's Johnny!"

The days which followed Johnny's new found sense of seeing his mama again and the joy which reflected on his face was a profound gift to all who cared for him. It does not matter how young one is, or what others may think when it comes to loss. Every human being experiences death, yet the very simple way of explaining the other side to Johnny brought immediate resolution of his loss.

WHEREVER YOU ARE, THEY ARE

Dalvin is an accomplished engineer who spends his time resolving problems and getting results. A few months after his mom passed away from lung cancer, Dalvin described the following experience to Maureen as "unusual and out of character for him." He has quite a sense of humor, but this was hard for him to tell anyone!

He was working on a job in Yakima, Washington, and

staying at his brother's home. One morning as he was taking a shower in the upstairs bathroom, he smelled cigarette smoke. He knew his brother did not smoke. No one in the family smoked, except his mom who had smoked her entire life. "There I was standing in the buff! I not only smelled smoke, but I turned and saw my mom sitting on the edge of the bathtub! She was wearing her red special-event dress. I said, 'Hi, Mom! How are you?' 'I am fine,' she said."

Dalvin described her as looking younger in appearance. There she was, perched on the edge of the bathtub, legs crossed, and smoking a cigarette. The second time he turned towards her, she was gone.

Dalvin dressed and went downstairs. He told his younger brother their mom had just visited him in the shower.

"What does she think of our new house?"

Dalvin replied, "I didn't ask."

Dalvin told Maureen he had never had anything like this happen in his life. He described the experience as being very real. He felt his mom had dropped in to check up on her sons. It took him many years before he shared this experience with someone other than a family member. Thinking that someone would question his experience or even deem it unreal, Dalvin carried this encounter with his mother around with him for years. His excitement was evident as he shared this story with Maureen.

Dalvin is just one clear example of individuals having an experience and feeling hesitant to share their experiences. It is so important for you to share these amazing encounters without fear. We are all connected to spirit.

The sharing of your own experiences can open the door for others to share theirs. Moments like these can open hearts and minds to the endless possibilities of their own connection to spirit.

FRED'S GOODBYE

It had been one of the days when Nola and Maureen had met to work on this book when they heard Fred's story. The hours of writing were often tedious and the need to take walks proved to be helpful. They were on their way back to the house when Nola recognized Joyce coming up the sidewalk towards them. There was a moment of hesitation before Nola moved to call out Joyce's name. At the same time she felt a need to spend a few minutes talking to Joyce. She knew Joyce worked as a professional guardian and this is how she had come to know her.

Nola introduced Joyce to Maureen, and Joyce asked what they were up to. Nola proceeded to tell Joyce they were working on a book. Joyce asked what the book was about. Nola discussed briefly the topic of the book. A surprised look came across Joyce's face. She smiled and then related the following story after disclosing she had never told anyone before.

"I was supervising a crew who were cleaning out an estate. While I was in the house, I received a phone message or I thought I did. The phone call was from my childhood friend, Fred. He lived out of state and would often call to talk to me. I answered the phone and saw his face as clearly as if he was standing here. It was round and smiling. 'I just wanted to say goodbye,' he said."

"I thought it was strange he only said goodbye and nothing else. When I returned home, I realized I hadn't actually received a phone call. It was a *waking dream* or *vision*. I still felt uneasy but comforted that I had seen his face. I checked my phone messages and found a message from a friend, telling me that Fred had fallen off a ladder pruning a fruit tree. He died as a result of the accident that same afternoon. While I still felt very unsettled by the experience, I took comfort in his coming to say goodbye to me."

To this day, whenever Joyce sees Nola she always says, "There isn't a day that goes by that I don't think about Fred."

Joyce described her last encounter with him as being in a waking dream. Perhaps for the two of them, spirit provided the perfect opportunity for the door between the two dimensions to open. We call this the space of no time. Those who experience this place will rarely ever forget it.

THE LATE NIGHT VISIT

George had lost his son at the young age of twelve in 1965. Clinton had died peacefully in his sleep after a struggle with cancer. It was very difficult for George to share his emotions over the loss of his son because he felt he had not taken the time when Clinton was alive to tell him how much he loved him. It was late that summer of 1965 when George had this late night visit.

Every night, George methodically checked to make sure the doors were locked, lights were out, and the swamp cooler turned off. (The swamp cooler was used in place of an air conditioner and was effective for cooling and humidifying homes in hot climates.) He would then go to bed. That night was no exception.

George was roused from his sleep during the night by the sound of the swamp cooler running. He got up out of bed and went to see what was going on. He walked into the living room and saw Clinton standing by the swamp cooler. George said, "You are welcome to stay as long as you need. I love you." He then proceeded to turn the swamp cooler off and went back to the bedroom.

It was many years before he shared this encounter. Shortly before his own death he told Nola about it.

It is never too late to tell someone how much you love them. Your words will always be heard. Sit quietly and set your intention. Speak from your heart and know that every heart-centered message sent out to the universe is received endlessly weaving its way through all dimensions.

No Warning

Clouds hang in the sky.
Waves toss on sandy shores.
Days melt into nights.
Death rocks our world.
Sometimes it arrives with no warning,
Our souls dissolving into other dimensions, like snowflakes,
Crystallizing, becoming one with the universe,
Renewed in the light and filled with the dawn of the day.
-Maureen McGill

CHAPTER 7:

OH, MAYBE?

Have you ever known individuals who live their lives on the edge? Most of us like to have some level of predictability in our lives. We develop daily routines without even noticing that in time we are just simply treading through life. These routines shape our temporary reality. This reality is predictable and many of us like the predictability. Then one day something very unpredictable happens. Our reality is shattered and then what?

Some will grasp the opportunity to experience the unpredictable. Others will simply shrug off what has taken place and continue to ignore the wake up calls. Events will continue to take place in life until one day the call of spirit is so strong it can no longer be ignored. Regardless of how these individuals choose their timing they eventually come to understand spirit always finds the perfect place and moment to grab our attention.

STEVE'S STORY

Steve and his partner Susan first met Paul and Linda at a school function for their children. The two couples shared much in common, and they had daughters the same age, Sophie and Jana. Over time Sophie's parents became like family to Steve, Susan, and their daughter Jana. Sophie had been born with a heart defect and also suffered from asthma. Typical of a young girl, she enjoyed spending her time with friends. The asthma never seemed to hold her back from participating in any of the activities she enjoyed. On just another seemingly normal day in Sophie's life, she was invited to spend the day at the amusement park with one of her close friends and her family.

The time at the amusement park passed quickly. Before everyone knew it, it was time to head home. No one could have anticipated the events which were to take place in the moments which followed leaving the park. The traffic was heavy and they found themselves in the midst of rush hour. Suddenly, Sophie went into one of her asthmatic episodes. No one could find her inhaler. It was impossible to access medical help in time. She did not survive the asthmatic attack.

The death placed Sophie's family and friends in shock. The family reached out to their friends for help and support. The days following her death were filled with making plans for the funeral service and the gathering afterwards.

Sophie's father asked Steve if he would stay after the service to be present when his daughter's casket was placed into the grave. Steve assured Paul he would stay.

The day of the funeral arrived. After the service Steve sensed the need to stay even after the casket had been lowered. He remained until well after dusk.

At the point when Steve knew it was time to leave, he walked back to his car, opened the door, and sat down. Shortly after placing the key in the ignition, he attempted to start the car, and the engine failed to turn over. Instead, the car radio began playing the song by Donna Lewis, "I Will Love You, Always Forever Near and Far, Close and Together." This was Sophie's favorite song. It continued to play over and over. This surprised Steve, but at the same time he recognized this to be a clear message from Sophie.

After the song had played a few times, he felt the need to say to her, "Sophie, I know it is you. I really need to get back to the house to be with your family. You will never be alone, *'We Will Love You, Always Forever.'*"

He sat in the car quietly for a moment before he realized what he had just said. Up until that moment, Steve had thought everything in life was concrete, three-dimensional, and that nothing existed, except his uniform, disciplined way of life. His reality was shattered when he realized he was talking to a dead person. He reacted by saying, "Oh boy! If anybody ever saw me talking aloud in the car alone, what would they think?" He attempted to start the car again. This time it started. He only shared this experience with Susan.

THE AWAKENING

Paul had built a career working in the medical field as a neurophysiologist. His specialty was centered on clients suffering from various types of brain injuries. He spent a tremendous amount of time thinking. Medicine and science work with facts and proven information which left very little time for Paul to explore the intuitive side of his brain. Often referred to as the right side, it is here where artists, writers and other people who work in the creative areas of industry develop their talents. The right side of the brain is often most developed in highly intuitive individuals. We call this intuitiveness "a knowing."

Paul and his wife Linda were first introduced to Steve and Susan through their daughter Sophie. Sophie's death at the age of eleven initiated a grieving process for Paul, encompassing a lengthy span of time.

He was visiting Steve and Susan a few years after Sophie's death. Paul knew Susan was intuitive and had shared with him various accounts and experiences with spirit or the other side. It goes without saying that every parent who has ever lost a child needs some form of reassurance, no matter what their belief system. Is their child okay? Is she/he safe? Is she/he with loved ones who have died before her/him? Can she/he hear us? Can they hear our messages and our attempts to talk to her/him? Is there some way she/he can give us a sign? How would we know if she/he was trying to contact us? What would it take for us to hear her/him?

Sophie's absence in Paul's life led him to eventually ask

Susan, "Do you feel Sophie around me?"

"Yes."

"How can I connect with her?"

She told Paul, "Set aside all judgment and fear. When you are completely present in the moment, you will open the portal for communication with Sophie."

Paul began to practice setting aside his judgments and fears. Once he had taken this step, he asked from his heart for a sign from Sophie. He set no expectations on how this communication would manifest and simply remained open to the moment. Then it happened!

One evening, he called Susan to tell her that he had been outside and saw two eagles circling overhead. This had caught his attention and he asked Susan, "What does that mean?"

Susan said, "In the world of Indian medicine the eagle represents Great Spirit."

A few days later, Paul called Susan again his voice was shaky, "I have been sitting outside and the two eagles came back. There was no wind, but the wind chimes behind me began to chime. It was at this moment I felt flooded with love, and I knew it was a message from Sophie. I could feel her and hear her."

This experience opened him to communicating with his daughter. This communication continues to this day.

Paul was able to step away from the scientific part of him. He grasped his own spirituality by allowing himself to recognize Sophie's presence. He helped create the conduit reaching between the two dimensions.

JILL'S MOTHER

Jill's mother was sixty-six years old, and she had been battling breast cancer for several years. Jill made it a habit to check in with her mother frequently. She and her husband, Frank, decided to go to their cabin in Canada for New Year's Eve without her mother. Her mom assured them she was quite all right at home by herself and wished them a Happy New Year!

On New Year's Day, Jill's daughter called to tell them her grandmother had suddenly taken a turn for the worse and was hospitalized. Jill and Frank returned to town and went directly to the hospital. They entered the room and saw the nurses caring for her mother, who was in a coma. Jill took one look at her and said to herself, "Mom, don't go now. Please don't go!"

She clearly heard her mother say, "Sweetie, I have to go now."

There was no way Jill's mother could have said any words aloud since she was in a coma, yet Jill felt this communication through her senses. Her mother did not often express affection and rarely called her "Sweetie." She took her mother's words as a sign it was time for her mother to go. Her mother died a short time later.

Six months after her mother's death, her father announced he was remarrying. Jill was not happy. She was sure her father had an affair with his soon-to- be bride during her mother's illness. A part of her wanted to show her father that she loved him, but at the same time she felt hurt by his action to remarry so soon. She could not bear to attend this family event.

Jill decided to take a nap on the day of the wedding. The thought of her father remarrying was too much for her emotionally. She was in a state between waking and sleeping when she heard her mother say. "I would never carry a grudge from the grave." Jill knew only her mother would say something like this. Her mother was a no-nonsense type of gal, and her words helped Jill to release all resentment toward her father in his new marriage. She attended the wedding after receiving the okay from her mother on the other side.

It is not uncommon for people who have had spouses die from a terminal illness or a long standing chronic disease to want to move forward in their lives. This desire to move forward is often misunderstood by their families. Few can understand the endless hours of caring, the silent wait and self-sacrifice. Some people wait years, and others often feel a need to move forward out of this dark period of their lives. It is hard for some family members to understand the loneliness of a surviving spouse. Why wouldn't you want him/her to experience love again? Do not force your agenda onto someone you love. It is only natural for humans to love. Unconditional love provides the perfect setting for us to heal and move forward in our lives.

AUDREY'S FATHER

Audrey was a neighbor of Maureen's for many years. They spent holidays together, cooking and laughing. Over time they came to know each other's family members whenever they visited from out of town.

Audrey's father had suffered from a series of strokes over a period of time. He lived in the Midwest while she resided on the West Coast. She traveled frequently to see him during the final months of his illness.

It was about a month after his death when Maureen had a dream about him. She found herself sitting at the dining room table in Audrey's house. Audrey had just finished setting the table with beautiful glasses, hand painted with deep purple violets.

In the dream Maureen called to Audrey, who was in the kitchen and asked, "How could you find the time to make this beautiful table setting and do all of this work?"

"Believe me, I had plenty of time. I did this awhile ago," she called from the kitchen as she continued working.

When Maureen turned back around, she saw Audrey's father sitting across the table from her. He looked different, much younger. Maureen said to him, "It's so nice to see you. I didn't have a chance to say good bye."

He said with his clear Bostonian accent, "That is okay, dear. I am busy now!"

Maureen asked, "Are you with Audrey's mom?" Audrey's mom had passed away a few years before her father.

"Oh yes, we are busy doing things."

This dream was important to Maureen. It offered an opportunity for her to say good-bye and to share with Audrey that her parents were together. Audrey was very disappointed she had not had a visit from her father and asked, "Why did Dad visit you instead of me?"

Maureen could feel Audrey's hurt and was hesitant to respond. She sensed the need to say, "It is hard to guess why some people have visits from their loved ones and why others never have this experience."

In a previous chapter we have discussed how sometimes it is easier for someone else to receive messages rather than those who are directly involved. When your heart is heavy, it is often hard to hear. You may be encompassed by the loss and still be trying to process your own grief.

Once again, those who cross come to realize that life goes on. They are now on the other side. The message you are sending is that they are dead! Hello! If you send out the message your father is dead/done/hit the big one, how in the world do you expect someone to talk to you?

Your emotions emit energy. Loss transmits as heavy energy instead of endless love which is a lighter energy. You have to release the loss to be open to the messages. This takes time for some while for others the need to release is natural and simply flows.

Maureen could not find the words to move Audrey through her loss. She recognized the need to share this experience with Audrey as a friend. There is an old saying, "It is what it is!" Sometimes words just simply cannot explain spirit.

Loss takes time for people to heal. Some people never get over the emotions of losing someone they love. They spend endless days engulfed in their feelings of loss; their hearts remain closed to the possibility their loved ones have left them. Perhaps,

61

it is a matter of finding a way to let go of the heaviness which people hold within themselves. Seeing a loved one pass is a rite of passage for all of us, and each individual may walk a different path during this time. There is no right way or wrong way. It is connecting with your heart in a new way that leads you forward.

HERE and HEREAFTER

Jodie was working in a Washington nursing home when her father was suffering from chronic congestive heart failure. She decided to go to California to be with her parents since her father's health had been failing for many months.

While she was in California, her father was hospitalized. During one of the family's visits at the hospital, her father said to them, "I want to go home."

Jodie's mother responded by saying, "Of course, you can go home!"

No one present during this conversation understood what he was saying. It wasn't until after the fact that Jodie realized her father was asking for permission to die. A few days later he passed.

Shortly after her father's death, all of the light bulbs in her parents' house started to burn out. The new television set went from a color picture to black and white. It didn't matter what anyone did to adjust the color, it remained the same. Jodie took these occurrences as signs from her father. Her mother was in such a state of grief that she did not notice at first. It was as if there was darkness, and the world turned black and white.

A few years later, her father's brother became terminally ill. During the course of his illness, Jodie became his primary care giver. Her uncle came to spend his last days living with her in her home.

Jodie's uncle and her father had been like two peas in a pod. They would play jokes on people and loved to play cards.

Shortly after her uncle's passing, Jodie went into what had been his room. The room was stone cold. She could hear voices and the shuffling of cards. The familiar voices were those of her deceased uncle and her father. She knew they were together again, carrying on as if nothing had ever happened.

This brought a smile to her face.

Jodie says there are times when she has to tell them to be quiet, so they won't wake her husband. There are times when she hears them in the kitchen, carrying on in the same manner as when they were alive. These encounters continue to bring joy into Jodie's life. She knows they have never left her.

You never know what will happen when you play your cards right!

CHAPTER 8:

CAN YOU BELIEVE THAT?

Some people are receptive to messages while others are not. Why? There are people who are born with very developed intuitive abilities. They learn how to pay attention to what they feel or sense and learn that how they feel may manifest in different ways. The right side of the brain is the intuitive and creative side where the messages are received. Heads and hearts are aligned. There are individuals who use their intuitive gifts to benefit and assist others in this world. Many of these individuals dedicate their lives to this work. Each and every individual has the ability to discover the wisdom of their own intuition.

HARLINE'S STORY

Harline was eighty-two years old when she faced the possibility of her own passing. She had not been feeling well at all. Cardiac problems had haunted her and this time was no exception. The chest pains from atrial fibrillation had made it a struggle to get through the day. She went to bed exhausted, still in pain.

During the night she had a dream. She saw herself standing on a sidewalk with her deceased husband, George. He was seventy-two years old when he passed. In the dream he appeared to be about twenty-nine years old. Harline looked across the street and saw the most beautiful green grass, then she looked up the street and saw a hill. Standing on the top of the hill was her deceased mother. To the immediate left of her mother was a field of flowers brilliant in color and like nothing she had ever seen.

Her mother waved to her. A strange silver colored vehicle

came down the street towards them and stopped in front of them. She recognized the driver as a long-time family friend, Kate, who had passed away several years earlier. Kate stepped out of the vehicle and they greeted each other. Harline does not remember all of her conversation with Kate, but she does remember telling Kate she wasn't ready to go and she was going back! Kate turned, stepped back into the vehicle and left.

Harline remembers raising her hand to wave good-bye to her mother and Kate,
right before she turned to ask George to get the car. She woke from this dream and the chest pain was gone. She told Nola it was as if she had been given a choice during the night: to continue living or to cross to the other side. She chose to stay.

Two years later Harline and Nola took a family vacation together. Nola asked her if she knew why she had decided it was not time for her to go. She said there were three things that she wanted to make sure occurred before she died. "I want my granddaughter to share her life with a man who will love and provide for her. I want my youngest son to have a good job and not have to struggle to make ends meet, and I want my book collection to go to someone who will love my books as much as I have loved them."

Harline had a choice to stay or depart. There are many individuals who have near death experiences. They relate hearing themselves or another voice say, "It is not time yet." These individuals often end up dramatically changed as a result of their experiences. This often serves as an awakening or a wake up call, another opportunity to continue to fulfill their life's purpose.

A PSYCHIC'S MESSAGES

Eric and Pat were married for more than thirty years. Eric struggled with his health, refusing to get a pacemaker, which eventually contributed to his death. It was some time after his death when Pat sought out a psychic; she wanted to talk to Eric.

Pat was shocked when the psychic began by saying, "He said to tell you he was such a pain in the ass!"

Pat started laughing and said, "That would be exactly what he would say."

The psychic said, "Eric says to tell you to give your son the ring which is in the drawer." Pat reassured the psychic she had given his son the ring. She thought about it for awhile and remembered another ring she had forgotten about in the dresser drawer. It was his class ring from his high school days.

"He also wants you to leave the picture on the wall that is hanging in the hallway. It is the one with the couple in the 1800 wedding garb." Pat was confused and couldn't remember any photos of relatives in the hallway.

When she returned home, she saw the photo. It was the same photograph the psychic had mentioned during the reading. This was a special photograph taken of Eric and Pat while they were on a trip shortly after their wedding. They had dressed in period costume garb and had such a good time. The photo helped her to reconnect to the memories and the feelings of times past.

Loved ones can connect to you in a soft and light-hearted way. Their messages can transform your grief and lift your hearts. Individuals who have the ability to connect with those who have crossed can be integral in helping people with their loss. They can connect with your loved one in such a way it will leave no doubt in your mind. You also can speak to them through your thoughts, dreams, and the very act of sending messages out from your heart. This isn't hard. It is as easy as sitting in your favorite chair and talking to your deceased Aunt Meg as if she were sitting right next to you.

A GIFT FROM HEAVEN

Jim's dad died in the Midwest a week before Christmas. He was close to his dad. His dad always thought Jim was talented at cooking and would make a great chef someday. Instead of becoming a chef, he became an acupuncturist and cranio-sacral therapist, but cooking became of his favorite hobby.

December 23rd was the wedding anniversary of Jim's parents and the date this experience occurred. He had recently moved from a house into a small apartment pairing down his belongings. It was late at night when Jim decided to take a much needed trip to the grocery store. There was four inches of fresh snow on the road. As he was driving home from the store, he came upon a large unwrapped box in the middle of the road. He stopped the car and walked over to the box. There were no markings on it or even a sign on the street of tire marks or footprints that someone had perhaps dropped the box. There was no evidence that the box had fallen off of a vehicle. He even checked the bushes nearby to see if someone had set the box there as a joke or needed assistance. The box appeared as if it had simply dropped out of the sky.

He picked up the box, placed it in his car and opened it. Inside of the box was a complete set of fancy cookware, pots and pans. Jim immediately felt his dad's presence. He was stunned as he knew his dad had always wanted him to be a chef. How could his dad know that he needed cookware for his new apartment? He had this overwhelming feeling this was his last Christmas gift from his dad.

UNEXPECTED DREAM VISITOR

Petra, a high school English and theatre teacher, had a remarkable dream about her deceased maternal grandmother who had died in 1996. It had been thirteen years since her death when her grandmother came to her for a visit in a dream.

They were in a cozy room with over-stuffed plush chairs and dark wooden tables, similar to the lobby of an old hotel in Canada or Europe. It was very warm and smelled of fresh flowers. Her grandparents always had amazing gardens and flowers where they were living. Petra loved to curl up in the midst of the garden with a book and coffee. She didn't remember actually seeing any flowers, but the fragrances were very powerful. Roses, lilacs, snapdragons, and sweet peas all intermingled. They were both seated at the start of their visit. Her grandmother pulled her chair closer and took Petra's hand in hers. This was something she did a lot when she was alive. She had the softest, most gentle hands. Even though her hands were arthritic and deformed, Petra distinctly remembered the undersides of her fingertips being smooth and soft. Her grandmother smelled of the perfume White Swan. She asked Petra how the "darlings were doing," that being her three children. Petra shared the good, bad and ugly of the three's latest travails. She responded with her usual laugh, covering her mouth when giggling hard. Petra thought she was always afraid her dentures would fall out. She would offer her small quips, "Oh, oh my gracious!"

"Do you like tea?" she asked.

"I love tea!" Petra answered.

Her grandmother proceeded to prepare a fruit and cheese plate. She continued the conversation, asking about her career as a teacher and director of theatre. She was always her greatest supporter and encouraged her to pursue dreams no matter how foolish they appeared to others. Her grandmother said, "All of your life experiences that you sometimes feel are holding you back are actually making your art better. Everything that you do with your heart makes your work more real and transparent."

Petra woke up feeling so happy, comforted and strengthened for living a few minutes in her presence. The encounter felt so completely tangible in every sense....and such a gift.

Visits
They come to us in all places.
They whisper, shout, and speak to us in waking moments.
They bring answers to wishes unspoken.
We need only to wait,
to trust,
to soften our hearts,
little by little,
day by day,
moment to moment.
-Maureen McGill

OUT OF THE FOG AND INTO THE NIGHT

Whitney worked in the emergency room of a local hospital in Central New York State. She lived in the country and often would travel to and from work in tandem with another nurse for support during inclement weather.

One particular day it had been raining, which made the evening drive home very foggy. Whitney and Tracey knew the trip home was going to be tricky due to poor visibility. Whitney was in the lead truck and Tracey was following in her car. When they came to a fork in the road where Whitney turned right and Tracey to the left, Whitney decided to follow Tracey to make sure she got home safely.

She was not breaking any land speed records and could hardly see to the end of the hood of her truck, but somehow she knew she was traveling downhill. Suddenly two columns of light appeared on either side of the front of her truck. She said, "What the heck!"

Right away she heard a female voice telling her, "Stay to the right." The voice repeated this several times. She did not recognize the voice as anyone she knew from her past or present. Once in a while, Whitney heard the same voice say, "Stay to the left," so she followed whatever directions the voice gave to her.

When they reached the bottom of the hill, the light disappeared, the fog faded, and they both went their own ways. Whitney felt spooked by this experience and spent most of the night questioning what had just happened.

The next day Whitney decided to take the same route back to work. She saw the road had been washed out, from the point that she first saw the columns of light all the way to the bottom of the hill. Whitney knew then that they had been protected from driving off the road into a deep ravine. The highway department had since closed the road for repairs. She knew this voice from out of the night had saved their lives.

Whitney was focused on being safe as she drove down the foggy road. She was not distracted by any head talk. This helped her be receptive to hearing the messages that came to her. To this day, she has no idea who the female voice was that guided her through the fog and into the night. There are those who believe that each one of us has a guardian angel. Perhaps it was Whitney's guardian angel who spoke that night.

IN DEATH WE DO NOT PART

Mary and Jim were married over fifty years. He became ill suddenly, and ended up dying. She was burdened with grief and also faced unsettled financial problems Jim had left to her.

Approximately one month after his death, Mary had a dream during an afternoon nap. There was a field carpeted in vibrant emerald green with a white fence. She could see a dimly lit barn. Then she saw Jim as she stepped into a closed room. He walked over to her and gave her a warm embrace. It felt real. Mary said to Jim, "You have to tell our lawyer that you are back."

Jim said clearly, "Not now." All this time he was embracing Mary. After a moment, he said to her, "Have you gotten any money yet?"

She said, "No."

He said, "It will be coming."

Mary awoke from the nap and went out to the mailbox to pick up the mail. A check from Jim's insurance company was in the box. She said it felt like a weight had been lifted from her shoulders. Her dream reassured her that Jim was okay and was with her even in death.

There have been other incidents of Jim communicating with her. She can be sitting in his recliner, relaxing, and suddenly can smell the familiar fragrance of his Old Spice cologne. She feels him lean up against the recliner; the cushion in the chair presses against her back just like old times.

At night, she knows he has come for a visit when suddenly she cannot pull the blankets up over her head. When he was alive, he would always tug and hog the blankets. She has even felt his warm hand touch the side of her leg; it is a sign he remains with her.

Always Here
My head rests in your arms.
These legs twist and wrap as edges melt.
Lips make hearts on necks of silken skin.
Hands hold heat of bodies speaking,
Transparent now, under blankets of
Clouds and limbs,
Under tears of sweetness and smiles.
Waking dreams caress moments in time.
-Maureen McGill

CHAPTER 9:

THAT'S CRAZY, BUT MAYBE?

DON'T BE SO STUBBORN!

Maria shared this story about three months after her friend Christina's death. She received a call from her daughter, Elena, who had been estranged from her family for sixteen years. Maria was raising Elena's children.

Elena called, unexpectedly to tell her mother that she had a strange dream about Christina, who was her godmother. This was her dream: "I saw Christina! She told me to tell you that she is okay. She wants you to know she is with you. Every time you see a flock of birds flying overhead, think of her. This is a sign Christina is giving you to let you know she is okay. She also said, 'Maria, don't be so stubborn!'"

Maria handed over the phone to Elena's daughter, who had not talked to her mother for many years. The daughter was excited at first to speak with her mother but then started crying. Elena lived in the East, far away from her family. At first Maria was very defensive, thinking this might be a trick of Elena's to make contact with her family, which she had abandoned many years earlier. She realized there was no way that Elena could know birds were a love of Christina's. Christina and Maria often watched the birds on the porch when she was alive.

Maureen and Maria discussed this dream. They talked about the possibility that Christina, Elena's godmother, was attempting to bring an end to the estrangement. It is not unusual for loved ones to assist in resolving unfinished business in this life. Your unfinished business is often their unfinished business. They pick up on the energy around our emotions because of the type of energy we are emitting. It is important to remember energy is a form of vibration. The emotional energy/vibration becomes their calling card. Often they will hang around attempting to get some type of resolution. Your resolution supports their evolution.

DANCING ON THE WAVES

Amy, age eighteen, had been estranged from her mother, Angela, for several years. Her parents divorced at an early age and Amy was raised mostly by her dad. Her mother's addictions and related behaviors drove Amy away. Her mother's lifestyle eventually led to her death in August 2003. Amy was not able to attend her funeral, but she did receive part of her mother's ashes to disperse in her own time. Her father had told Amy that her mother once mentioned if she died, she wanted her ashes scattered in the ocean near Carlsbad, California.

It took Amy two years to part with her mother's ashes. She said, "I couldn't let her go." She finally had the courage to make her mother's wish come true. Amy and a friend headed to the California coast and were staying in Laguna Beach. When they arrived at Carlsbad they noticed the ocean was neon, the waves would crest in this iridescent crystal blue color.

"I stared out into the ocean and was in total awe of the beauty of the waves as I scattered the ashes. I felt so much peace and closure. As I stood there, I swear to this day I saw a youthful figure dancing on top of the waves. It looked like an outline of a woman with her hair flowing, as though she was dancing upon the waves and spinning in circles. She looked free, happy and with so much joy in her face! I felt so elated! I knew it was my mother!"

Amy and her friend started walking down the beach and paused to ask a couple, "Do you know why the ocean is such a vibrant blue today? We have never seen anything like it."

"It is a red tide. This happens occasionally here on the

coast, it is the neon phytoplankton in the waters."

As a professor of biological sciences at UCSD, Peter Franks, wrote in response to swimming in the red tide, "Your hands will glow in front of you, and you will be covered in tiny glowing stars when you come out of the water."

Amy and her mother both found freedom within the magical glow of the waters on that day.

> *Stars melt over bodies of silken ashes*
> *Dancing in circles of light and neon,*
> *Mothers, fathers, sons and daughters*
> *Spirits rise to skies of stars and moon.*
> *Grief dissolves within luminescent waters of blue.*
> *-Maureen McGill*

LET IT RIP

Marsha's grandmother cared for her from birth. When Marsha was seven, her grandmother passed away. After her death Marsha always felt her grandmother's presence close to her. Several years elapsed and Marsha grew from a young child into a young woman.

In her early twenties, she began exclusively dating a very abusive man. Eventually she became pregnant and gave birth to a baby boy. Her boyfriend's abuse escalated to the point where a restraining order was obtained to protect her and the baby from any further violence. The baby's father made a decision to make this a custody battle. Because the father's name did not appear on the birth certificate, the court ordered a DNA test. The court order did not upset Marsha because she knew beyond doubt that he was the father of her child.

It was the day before the custody hearing when Marsha was driving home alone down a country road. Her cell phone rang, and it was her ex-boyfriend, screaming, "I am going to take the baby away from you!" This was accompanied by a series of obscenities and open ended threats.

Marsha was so frustrated she screamed aloud, "Whatever happens, let it rip!"

It was at that moment when she looked in her rearview mirror. In the back seat was sitting her deceased grandmother Rosemary. She looked the same as Marsha had remembered as a child. She had soft curls and was wearing glasses. Her grandmother spoke to her, "Mazzie, (Marsha's nickname), it is going to be okay. I blew up the engine in his truck, and the DNA test will be negative. He is not the dad, and you do not have to worry." Marsha started to cry.

The next day the results of the DNA test confirmed he was not the father. Two days later Marsha found out that his car engine had failed, and he was not injured. She could hardly believe what had happened. She showed Nola and Maureen the court report that showed the DNA test as negative. The whole situation was a miracle to her. She was absolutely amazed at the power of her own words. The appearance of her grandmother, and the events which led up to the resolution of the child custody battle seemed like a miracle to her.

Marsha surrendered to the moment through her own words, "Whatever happens, let it rip." Her words stated an intention. She was no longer going to attempt to control the situation or the outcome. Letting go opened the door for her grandmother to help her in a very miraculous way. To this day, she considers her grandmother's appearance as a miracle.

We believe we are spiritual beings coming to this earth to live and participate in the development of our souls. Often we forget how connected we are to each other, no matter where we are. Requesting help is only a matter of thinking it, asking aloud or simply setting the intention that someone could help us.

IN THE ARMS OF AN ANGEL

April was eighty-three at the time she shared her story. She had married at a young age and had three children. Her husband had died unexpectedly of non-Hodgkin's lymphoma when they were both still young. She had loved him dearly.

It was about a year after her husband's death when April began dating another man. Not long after they started dating, she discovered she was pregnant with his child. The thought of bringing this child into the world seemed overwhelming to her as a single mother. All of her fears and worries came to the surface.

One night she had a dream. In the dream her deceased husband handed her a beautiful pink bundle, which contained a baby girl. "She is beautiful," he said. April awoke from the dream knowing it was okay to have the baby. All feelings of being overwhelmed and fearful had vanished. She interpreted the significance of her husband handing the baby girl to her, as his blessing of the unborn child. Her daughter is now forty-six and lives with April.

Waking Dreams of You
My heart tangled in your hair,
This body smooth wraps around you.
Your words turn to ruby sparks on your throat.
Where is love that holds this memory?
It is sealed in secret kisses, in envelopes of dreams.
-Maureen McGill

JIM'S DREAMS

Maureen has known Jim for over fifteen years. He moved to the Midwest out of a need to be closer to his aging parents. Eventually Jim's father passed away. Jim's first visit from his father occurred two years later in the form of a dream.

Jim was at an alligator park. The alligator pits were surrounded by low chicken wire fences to keep them from escaping. As he stood watching the alligators he noticed a man standing with his back to him. The man was wearing a park ranger cap, similar to the baseball caps his dad had always worn. He knew it was his dad.

"Dad, what are you doing here?" Jim asked.

He replied, "I'm so happy here. I'm doing a job that is fun!" During his life, he was not happy with his job as a mechanic. "Here I can talk to people and animals all day. Let me get us both some popcorn and a Coke. We better get out of here soon because, when the pits fill up with water, the alligators will crawl out."

They walked over to a car that Jim recognized as a car his dad owned when he was younger. His dad said, "Get in the car and go down this road."

When they arrived at the T-intersection, Jim asked, "Left or right?"

His dad said, "Go straight."

"Is that okay, Dad?," he asked, "This is a park road." They were driving over grass, and the grass turned into the Great Plains with buffalo walking past the car. "Where are we going, Dad?," Jim asked.

"We're going west," his dad said. "Go west!" They traveled over the Great Plains and eventually ended in the Rocky Mountains. They could not drive the car any farther.

They climbed the mountains together ending up in Washington State where they used to live. In the last part of the dream Jim remembered being in the back of a salmon hatchery where there was water in front of him. It was at this point that he woke up with a profound sense of peacefulness. He knew this was a visit from his dad, and he was very happy knowing his dad was finally content.

That same evening Jim went back to sleep, and this time he had a dream about his sister who had died the year before from a brain aneurysm. In the dream, the phone rang. He answered it and heard his sister say, "Jim, the house is empty. I need you to help me find my bobby pins and some chocolate-covered cherries."

Shortly after her death, the family had cleared out her house. They found lots of bobby pins all over the place. Jim said, "When we were kids, my sister would be sent to the store for bread. She would use the leftover change to buy chocolate-covered cherries. Once home, she hid them under her bed. When the timing was just right, she would call me into her room and share the chocolate-covered cherries with me."

In the dream, Jim heard himself say to his sister over the phone, "We thought you were dead! That is why we got rid of everything."

She said, "No, I've just been in a coma! The doctors didn't want to get everyone's hopes up, so they told you I was dead." Jim started to go to the store for her just before he woke up. He felt comforted by her presence.

Jim woke from his dream feeling good having spoken to his sister once again. He had not had a chance to say goodbye before she died. Later on when he shared this dream with Maureen, he expressed his concern that his sister had not acknowledged she had passed away. She came across to him as confused. He told Maureen he was going to include his sister in his meditations with the hopes it would help her move forward, knowing all of her personal affairs were in order.

We all hold beliefs and perceptions. These perceptions can go as deep as your philosophical beliefs, theological beliefs, etc. Some of us within our lives have situations and encounters that alter these beliefs. The same is true when we transition. Jim's sister had not yet acknowledged her own death. In the dream she had portrayed her passing as the physicians' belief.

The physical world in which we live in is the only dimension where time exists. It is our belief when individuals transition, they lose all sense of time and space. She still carried with her the energy of this lifetime. This energy affected her transitioning from one dimension to the other. It is not just as easy as the saying, "Here one day and gone the next."

Even on the other side, we continue clearing the energy from this lifetime. The transition of one's soul provides the opportunity to heal and to recognize we are one with the divine. Jim's intention to help his sister through meditating opened the door to the light. It is within the divine where we can reach, united, to assist even those who have passed.

CHAPTER 10:

OH, FOR HEAVEN'S SAKE!

Have you ever thought about the intuitive capacity of young children? Long before they can speak, they sense love, comfort, and danger without necessarily experiencing this before. Children continue to remain intuitive until their minds become steeped by this scientific world we live in. There are some children who continue to develop their intuitive gifts well into their adult years. These gifts become a part of their everyday life and, in certain circumstances, protect them far beyond the reaches of the rational mind.

A CHILD'S WALK DOWN THE AISLE

Carson was not quite two years of age when his father, Craig, was tragically hit by a car and killed at the age of thirty-seven. Craig had a very easy going disposition. He was hard-working, fun-loving, and always had time to help people.

The day of his memorial service arrived. The church was filled with those who had come to pay their final respects. Craig had been a member of the local emergency fire services. Fire departments and emergency services have garnered the tradition of *The Ringing of the Bell.*

The members of the local emergency services all rose and moved to the right side of the podium as the Chief of the fire department walked up to the front and placed a large bell upon the lectern. He shared with all present the symbology of ringing the bell: "The bell is to be rung three times; the final ring confirms the death of a firefighter."

The fire chief rang the bell for the first time. Little Carson started walking up the aisle of the church toward the back. His hands were folded behind his back. He moved from one side of the aisle to the other side, one row at a time. He extended his hand to shake the hand of each person sitting on the aisle seat. It was amazing to watch this small child so intent, not skipping a single person. It was as if Craig was present with his son, walking him gently up the aisle.

The bell rang for the third time. Precisely at that moment, the child turned and began walking back down the aisle towards the podium. He paused in front of his father's portrait before he returned to his chair. Craig's toddler son did exactly as Craig would have done. It was as if Craig's spirit was acknowledging all who had come to celebrate his life with the help of Carson, who had extended his hand to everyone, even if he didn't know them.

There are signs and symbols around us all the time. When you are truly present to the moment, you will connect to the subtle messages those that have passed convey to us.

TIME FOR COFFEE

Madeline was a resident of a nursing home. Nola would visit her every Friday afternoon. Madeline enjoyed a ritual of having coffee and homemade cookies and reminiscing with Nola about family and friends. Eventually, Nola was transferred to another facility within the company. Madeline gave her an exquisite tea cup as a parting gift.

Periodically, Nola would visit Madeline on her day off. Time elapsed, and a nurse informed Nola that Madeline was not doing well; she was failing quickly. Nola received a call asking if she would come to say good-bye. It was about 10:30 A.M. when Nola arrived at the facility. Madeline's children were in the room. She had been failing for several days, and the family couldn't figure out why their mother was continuing to hold on.

Nola went over to the bedside, knelt down on the floor next to her bed, and put her left hand on Madeline's left arm. She told Madeline she came to say good-bye and assured her it was okay to let go. Nola told Madeline that her family was distressed and wanted to know if there was anything that was holding her back. Madeline was in and out of consciousness.

She was a devout Catholic, and Nola asked one of her daughters if Madeline had been given the Last Rites yet. Kaye assured Nola she had been given the rites several days prior. Nola continued to sit in stillness with Madeline. Silently Nola asked herself, "What is holding her back?" She looked up and saw that is was Friday on the calendar. She immediately remembered Friday and their Friday routine. They had always shared coffee and cookies together.

Nola announced to the family they were all going to have coffee with Madeline today. The coffee arrived and while they were all sipping, Madeline's breathing began to change. When they had finished their coffee, Nola went back over to the bed and told Madeline they were done. Nola knelt down next to the bed, put her hand on Madeline's left arm, and asked her if there was anything else they needed to do for her.

Nola felt the need to recite the Lord's Prayer. As everyone said the last sentence of the prayer, Madeline took her final breath. It was a sacred moment for everyone.

Nola followed her intuition. Those final hours of everyone coming together was a culmination of certain things important to Madeline in her life.

When somebody you love is dying, ask yourself what you can do for them. How can you hold this very precious space while they make their transition? It is an honor to be with someone when he/she is dying even though it is hard for us. Allow yourself to feel the silence and connect with him/her intuitively.

There is sacredness in helping an individual cross over. The connection between each soul present in the room held the space for Madeline. The veil between the dimensions opened, allowing Madeline to move forward.

A DAUGHTER'S LOVE

Phyllis's mother lived with her family for the last fifteen years of her life. Phyllis was outside watering the roses in her garden before she entered the house to find her mother unconscious on the floor. Her three dogs were whining and pushing with their noses, trying to get her mother to respond. She cradled her mother in her arms, telling her how much she loved her and how much her mother meant to her, as Phyllis added, "This time around."

Her daughter called for medical help and remained beside her mother placing a pillow under her head. She told her mother if this was truly her time to go, she would understand. As Phyllis was holding her mother, she saw a golden glowing light rise out of her mother's body and stand beside her. She felt her mother's love enveloping her as she said goodbye. This golden light took the shape of her mother. The light shape turned away from Phyllis, moved out the back door to the garden, up the steps and into an opening of brilliant white light.

Phyllis followed her mother's wishes to be cremated. She wanted her ashes to be spread over the Blue Ridge Mountains, close to the birds and animals she loved. The day came for Phyllis to fulfill her mother's wish. As they ascended the mountain, Phyllis and her daughter came upon a viewing area. They decided this sight was where the ashes should be scattered. Just as they stepped out of the car holding the urn, a red-tailed hawk appeared and began circling over their heads. The hawk cried out when they gently began to spread the ashes and then flew away.

They got back into the car and began their descent down the mountain road. They encountered a black bear who ambled out of the woods by the roadside. The bear stopped and turned to stare at the car, paused, and then returned to the woods. Everyone in the car remarked on the appearance of the hawk and bear. Phyllis felt these were a sign her mother was with them.

BLANKET OF LIGHT

At eighty-nine years of age, Opaline had resided in a Cashmere, Washington nursing home for about six years. She had only one daughter, Harline. The day Opaline died, her daughter was called to the nursing home and sat with her mother for some time.

Early in the evening it started getting dark. Harline sat beside the bed with her hand next to her mother's hand. She became aware of a light starting to fill the room and realized the lights in the room had not been turned on. The glow started out as white and as it filled the room, the colors transformed to the most beautiful yellow and orange. The colors emitting from the light engulfed the bed. Harline felt like she had been wrapped up in a warm flannel blanket. The warmth created a sense of peace and calm. She didn't know how many minutes passed before she saw the light begin to recede from the room. It moved from the bottom of the bed all the way to the top of the bed, and then vanished. She knew at that moment her mother had passed.

Harline remains forever touched by the peacefulness, calm, and absolute beauty of the light which she experienced on the day her mother passed.

WHERE DO WE GO FROM HERE?

Final Thoughts

The stories contained in this book have revealed to our readers the concept of "it is not over, when you think it is over." Your thoughts and feelings are always known to those on the other side. All of us have the ability and will be provided with opportunities to connect with those who have passed in our lifetime. These experiences will help us to acknowledge that physically dead does not mean gone forever.

There will be times when you may feel that you are very alone in this world. This feeling can be overwhelming shortly after the loss of someone you have loved. We long to hear their voice again, touch them again or hold them again. The unspoken words which we may not have shared with them resounds within us and our regrets can hold us hostage.

All of us are connected within this universe. The universal connection is like a sacred thread which serves as a conduit. It is never too late to share your feelings, thoughts and words whether consciously or unconsciously with those who have passed. This thread acts like a telephone line sending your messages out into the universe. Remember, at some point a response will be sent to you. Their response may come in different forms; dreams, visions, voices, electronic devices, or nature.

When the calling card is sent to you, will you be willing to answer?

Our book has served as a vehicle for many on this side to share their stories and encounters with the other side. It is our hope that some day you will also have the courage and desire to share your own story. You may never know who you will help or how your story will impact them. It is a powerful moment when you find your voice and tell others about your experience. Those on the other side have a wish to be heard. Our love for each other knows no boundaries.

In The Beginning

In the beginning we are of the light.
The light is within us and surrounds us.
We journey forth as light moving into earth time and
space to the moment of our birth, this soul's journey.
Then comes the call,
the reminder, the longing of our true essence.
This calls our soul to come home.
On earth we know this as death.
In the universe it is the movement, to be once again in
and
of
the
light.

-Nola Davis

About the Authors

Maureen McGill, MA, BFA, is an Associate Professor of Theatre/Dance at Pacific Lutheran University in Tacoma, Washington. She directs the university dance ensemble and teaches courses in dance, movement and choreography. Healing Arts of Mind and Body is a course she has designed which focuses on alternative healing, energy medicine and body modalities. Meditation, Relaxation and Dance workshops are part of her passions, where she also teaches at the Breast Cancer Resource Center in the Tacoma/Seattle region.

Maureen's keen interest in the intuitive arts has expanded her curiosity to the spiritual side of life and death. She is a featured reader of tarot and appears at Intuitive Arts Fairs in the Seattle region. As a frequent guest on local and international radio networks, her work has opened doors using symbols and metaphors to help those find light in the midst of loss and grief.

Maureen enjoys the beauty of the Pacific Northwest where she lives with her daughter. For more information regarding Maureen go to her website: www.livefromtheotherside.com

Nola Davis, CEO, NHA, has spent the last thirty-three years working in the senior healthcare industry. Working with the elderly helped lay the foundation for her desire to understand the spiritual aspects of death. Her work as a healthcare administrator provided the opportunity to understand hospice and involve hospice services within the facilities where she worked. As a CEO of a healthcare corporation, she now aspires to bring integrative services which support the body, mind and soul into the every day realm of healthcare. She has studied Healing Touch with Healing Touch International as well as other facets of the world of complimentary medicine.

Nola lives with her husband in the Pacific Northwest. For more information regarding Nola go to her website at www.livefromtheotherside.com

Other Books Published
by
Ozark Mountain Publishing, Inc.

Continue for more books by Ozark Mountain Publishing, Inc.

For more information about any of the above titles, soon to be released titles, or other items in our catalog, write or visit our website:

OZARK
MOUNTAIN
PUBLISHING

PO Box 754
Huntsville, AR 72740
www.ozarkmt.com
1-800-935-0045/479-738-2348
Wholesale Inquiries Welcome